NEW DIRECTIONS FOR TEACHING

Robert E. Young, *University of Wisconsin*
EDITOR-IN-CHIEF

Learning Communities: Creating Connections Among Students, Faculty, and Disciplines

Faith Gabelnick
Western Michigan University

Jean MacGregor
The Evergreen State College

Roberta S. Matthews
City University of New York

Barbara Leigh Smith
The Evergreen State College

Number 41, Spring 1990

JOSSEY-BASS INC., PUBLISHERS
San Francisco

Learning Communities: Creating Connections Among Students, Faculty, and Disciplines.
Faith Gabelnick, Jean MacGregor, Roberta S. Matthews, Barbara Leigh Smith.
New Directions for Teaching and Learning, no. 41.

NEW DIRECTIONS FOR TEACHING AND LEARNING
Robert E. Young, Editor-in-Chief

Copyright © 1990 by Jossey-Bass Inc., Publishers

NEW DIRECTIONS FOR TEACHING AND LEARNING is part of The Jossey-Bass Higher Education Series and is published quarterly by Jossey-Bass Inc., Publishers. Second-class postage paid at San Francisco, California, and at additional mailing offices. Postmaster: Send address changes to Jossey-Bass Inc., Publishers, 350 Sansome Street, San Francisco, California 94104.

EDITORIAL CORRESPONDENCE should be sent to the authors c/o Jossey-Bass Inc., Publishers, 350 Sansome Street, San Francisco, California 94104.

Jossey-Bass Web address: http://www.josseybass.com

Library of Congress Catalog Card Number LC 85-644763
International Standard Serial Number ISSN 0271-0633
International Standard Book Number ISBN 1-55542-838-X

Cover photograph by Richard Blair/Color & Light © 1990.

Contents

PREFACE

We set out to write a book that describes a special approach to curriculum reform: learning communities. We intend to introduce interested and curious educators to learning community concepts, strategies, and outcomes. Those who have already participated in learning communities will enjoy sharing the familiar perceptions and data we have collected. We name institutions and different types of learning communities not to promote them but rather to inform the reader about the programs and institutions that are leaders in the learning community network. We suspect that many more programs on college campuses are not labeled "learning communities" but have many of the characteristics we describe. We invite those readers who say "We've been doing this for quite a while" to write to us and send us their materials. Learning communities are, after all, a generic term for a variety of curricular interventions. Our task has not only been to identify commonalities but also to encourage variation among the next group of learning community leaders.

Like most reformers, we have had to do battle with Zeal, that blinding, imperious force that changes deliberation into a crusade. We believe that learning communities are an appropriate, rational, and ethical response to many challenges in higher education. Yet we constantly need to remind ourselves that learning communities are not a panacea, that they are not preferred universally, and that they are not a quick fix for a campus. Still, zeal has a way of creeping in.

During our work sessions we struggled to maintain our own ideas, to consider new approaches, and to be open to each other's criticisms and revisions. In a word, we formed a learning community, valuing the individual while cherishing collaboration. As we searched for common ground and a shared language, our understanding of each other deepened and clarified. Imperceptibly, our ideas, our words, began to blend. In a real sense, then, this book is more than any of us could have written alone, wiser than any one mind, and stronger because we never gave in.

Learning Communities: Creating Connections Among Students, Faculty, and Disciplines presents the process of conceiving, implementing, teaching, and reflecting on learning communities. It offers a complex picture of the dynamic and evolving learning community environment. Ideally, this volume ought to be read in one sitting so that the images and information from each chapter move back and forth and build on each other.

Chapter One describes some major educational innovators whose legacy is the concept of the learning community. We set these remarks in a contemporary context to remind our readers that learning communities are a timely educational intervention and that they have firm roots in both individualistic and collaborative educational theory. In fact, it is this tension between the needs of the individual and the larger group that is at the heart of the learning community ethos.

Over the years, five generic frameworks of learning communities have evolved. In Chapter Two we describe these models, reminding and encouraging our readers to adapt them to their own institutional needs.

How to create, implement and sustain learning communities is the focus of Chapter Three. The process of innovation is described in detail to prepare those who wish to begin a learning community. Creating learning communities is in itself a community-building experience wherein the academic institution becomes an overarching network of support for a complicated enterprise.

The experience of learning and teaching in learning communities can transform one's ideas about undergraduate education and faculty development. Chapter Four looks at the issue of what learning communities ask of teachers and students and how the different models affect pedagogy.

The outcomes, from student and faculty perspectives, are extraordinary. In Chapter Five we describe the students who join learning communities, what they say about their experience, and what we know about the impact of learning communities. This format is mirrored in Chapter Six, in which faculty recount rejuvenating intellectual and social encounters with students and colleagues. They bask in community support; they reflect on their own professorial history and find, with some surprise, that learning communities offer an unparalleled opportunity for enrichment, empowerment, and connection.

In Chapter Seven we look outward to broader issues in higher education and again connect our major themes to the challenges facing the nation today. It is no accident that we again emphasize the important and fundamental dialectic between individual agendas and the life of the community.

Chapter Eight presents information on additional resources about learning communities. In addition to providing a brief bibliography, we present a list of networks and contact persons in schools with learning communities. This chapter is not intended to be exhaustive but merely suggestive of other resources and groups whose focus is either contained in or expanded by the learning community.

In writing this book, we have drawn on the generosity of many people who shared their programs and their ideas about teaching and learning. In interviews, journals, and evaluations, hundreds of faculty and administrators and thousands of students expressed their enthusiasm and commitment. Particular thanks go to learning community faculty, administrators, and students at SUNY at Stony Brook, The Evergreen

State College, Rollins College, La Guardia Community College, University of Tennessee, The University of Maryland College Park Honors Program, Babson College, The Carl and Winifred Lee Honors College at Western Michigan University, Stockton State College, the Quanta Program at Daytona Beach Community College, and the Integrated Studies Program at the University of North Dakota. Special notice is also given to those dozens of institutions that form the Washington Center for the Improvement of Undergraduate Education, especially The Evergreen State College and Seattle Central Community College, for their early leadership in establishing learning communities throughout Washington state.

Many individuals helped us think more clearly about what we do. These educators and innovative leaders in higher education are also friends and colleagues. We are deeply fortunate to know them and to have their support. Among those with whom we work closely are Rob Cole, Zelda Gamson, Patrick Hill, John Howarth, Anita Landa, Jerri Lindblad, David Paulsen, Karen Romer, Sharon Rubin, Jill Mattuck Tarule, and William Whipple. Special thanks go to Marian Arkin, Susan Forman, Gail Green, George Groman, Lucia Harrison, Mark Levensky, Bob Matthews, and Rita Phipps Smilkstein, who read and criticized this manuscript. Roberta Floyd and Laura O'Brady patiently typed and retyped this manuscript with their usual dedication and high standards of excellence. Mark Clemens deserves special credit for editing the final manuscript. All of these people are members of a national learning community network, and all are characterized by their inventiveness and patience, their respect for their colleagues, their students, and themselves. In a special way, this book belongs to them all.

Faith Gabelnick
Jean MacGregor
Roberta S. Matthews
Barbara Leigh Smith

Faith Gabelnick is dean of The Carl and Winifred Lee Honors College at Western Michigan University.

Jean MacGregor is associate director of the Washington Center for Improving the Quality of Undergraduate Education at The Evergreen State College.

Roberta S. Matthews is associate dean for academic affairs and professor of English at LaGuardia Community College, City University of New York.

Barbara Leigh Smith is academic dean and director of the Washington Center for Improving the Quality of Undergraduate Education at The Evergreen State College.

*Learning communities address modern problems but trace their
roots to earlier twentieth-century reform movements.*

Learning Community Foundations

> Every institution of higher learning should create learning
> communities organized around specific intellectual themes
> or tasks.
>
> —National Institute of Education
> *Involvement in Learning*, 1984

Many colleges are creating learning communities as an avenue of educational improvement and faculty revitalization. In a time of widespread criticism of higher education, learning communities constitute an unusual reform effort because of their focus on the structural features of our institutions and our curriculum as both the problem *and* the solution.

Although there are many different types of learning communities and the term itself is very broad, this analysis focuses on a distinctive type of learning community. Learning communities, as we define them, purposefully restructure the curriculum to link together courses or course work so that students find greater coherence in what they are learning as well as increased intellectual interaction with faculty and fellow students. Advocates contend that learning communities can address some of the structural features of the modern university that undermine effective teaching and learning. Built on what is known about effective educational practice, learning communities are also usually associated with collaborative and active approaches to learning, some form of team teaching, and interdisciplinary themes.

In addition to reviewing the work of the most significant modern learning community theorists, Alexander Meiklejohn and John Dewey, this chapter shows how learning communities are a timely response to contemporary issues in higher education. Dewey believed that we live in

NEW DIRECTIONS FOR TEACHING AND LEARNING, no. 41, Spring 1990   © Jossey-Bass Inc., Publishers the present and that to prepare for the future it is important to extract the full meaning of the present. In this connection, we review the major issues raised in recent higher education reports. Learning communities provide a means of addressing a broad array of these issues simultaneously. By understanding why learning communities are successful, we can gain important insights into the process of educational reform. We may, at the same time, come to see "the issues" in a somewhat different light.

Recent Critiques of Higher Education

In the past fifteen years, there has been an outpouring of pessimism about America's educational system. The discussion initially focused on the K–12 system, prompted by the influential report *A Nation at Risk*, and then shifted to postsecondary education through a myriad of other national and state reports (see Association of American Colleges, 1985; Study Group on the Conditions of Excellence in Higher Education, 1984). The larger public was brought into the debate with the publication of a number of best-selling books, including Allan Bloom's *The Closing of the American Mind* (1987), E. D. Hirsch's *Cultural Literacy* (1987), Dianne Ravitch's *What Our Seventeen-Year-Olds Don't Know* (1988), and Charles Sykes's *ProfScam: Professors and the Demise of Higher Education* (1988). Questions were asked about the content of the curriculum, about who is teaching the nation's undergraduates, and about how faculty spend their time. At the state level, issues are being raised about educational quality and declining standards, about educational accountability, and about the way the higher education system is organized. Parents and legislators alike are probing what students are learning and not learning, why the attrition rate is so high, and why higher education seems to fail students in so many ways. Special concern in these recent reports has focused on the faculty, the curriculum, and the changing nature of the students in our institutions. Brief reviews of these concerns will provide a backdrop for our argument that learning communities are a vehicle for responding to all of these issues at once.

Faculty. A number of recent reports center on the faculty and the quality of life in our institutions (Bowen and Schuster, 1986; Boyer, 1987; Seidman, 1985; Astin, 1985). They describe an aging, largely immobile, and often demoralized faculty, a faculty who feel underappreciated and underpaid. In *American Professors: A National Resource Imperilled* (1986) Bowen and Schuster contend that the past fifteen years were especially difficult because major gains in compensation and faculty influence over academic policy were interrupted and reversed.

Ernest Boyer's Carnegie Commission study, *College: The Undergraduate Experience in America* (1987), reports that nearly half of the nation's faculty would move to nonacademic positions if given the opportunity, and more than half rate the intellectual atmosphere in their institution as "fair" or "poor." Earl Seidman's 1985 study of community college faculty reaches similar conclusions. Concentrating on the conflict between the liberal and vocational arts, the diffuse mission of the community college, and the obstacles to effective teaching, Seidman, like the others, suggests that creative ways must be found to restore the intellectual vitality of the faculty. Howard Bowen (1985) looks at the issue of enhancing educational quality in financial terms and suggests that the cost of effective educational reform may well be beyond our reach.

Many of the recent reports criticize the way we prepare and reward faculty and the decline of teaching as a significant and valued activity. As Boyer puts it, "many of the nation's colleges are more successful in credentialing than in providing a quality education for their students. It is not that the failure of the undergraduate college is so large but that the institutional expectations are often so small" (1987, p. 2).

Bowen and Schuster, Boyer, and Astin all recommend a more diversified reward system that recognizes the value of teaching and the undergraduate experience. They also contend that we must recognize our diversity and the reality that most of our institutions are not focused primarily on graduate training. In the face of an increasingly specialized, discipline-centered faculty, special issues then arise about reforming undergraduate education and encouraging the kind of sustained commitment on the part of individual institutions that this reform will require.

In "The Way We Think Now: Ethnography of Modern Thought," Clifford Gertz speaks of the "extremely peculiar career pattern that marks the academic disciplines: namely, that one starts at the center of things and then moves towards the edges" (Gertz, 1983, p. 158). The problem of building community and commitment is exacerbated by this "peculiar" career pathway. What Gertz calls the faculty's "exile from Eden syndrome" contributes to the current dilemma in academic life. Many colleges cannot hope to duplicate the specific, disciplinary richness of graduate education nor does graduate training equip most faculty to step comfortably outside disciplinary boundaries. The result is often a kind of intellectual isolation at the home institution, which must offer its faculty alternative growth opportunities to counteract the frustrations of disciplinary diaspora. The lack of local opportunities for community building, professional development, and experimentation may increase the sense of disengagement on the part of the faculty. The infinite variety of colleges and universities further increases the lack of communication and dissipates any sense of shared goals among institutions. Ironically, both within and among colleges, faculty lack opportunities to learn from one another at precisely the moment when increasing communication among diverse faculty has become a necessity.

Looking to the future, issues are being raised about how we will replenish our ranks in the approaching era of large-scale retirements, especially when the profession is declining in status. The situation will become increasingly acute. One-third of higher education's professoriate will retire within the next ten to fifteen years, and within twenty-five years the entire faculty of 700,000 will replace itself.

Curriculum. Concern about the condition of the faculty is mirrored by concern about the curriculum. Running in tandem with dour reports about job satisfaction in higher education are an array of writings that point to a crisis in the curriculum. The twin issues of curricular coherence and curricular rationale loom large. While Bloom chides us for turning our backs on what he defines as our major traditions, Hirsch takes us to task for not identifying and introducing our students to the catchwords of our culture (Bloom, 1987; Hirsch, 1987). For every champion of Western civilization, another arises to criticize a view of the "canon" that is too narrow. Particularly vociferous criticism has come from those in the academy arguing for a more inclusive, multicultural, gender-balanced, global perspective. One solution, offered by Gerald Graff, suggests that we "teach the debate" over the canon instead of trying to resolve it through narrow definitions (1986, 1987).

Arguments about the traditional curriculum are acute in the nation's community colleges. Here the introduction of new areas of learning, many of them linked to the job market, serves only to complicate an already complex curricular equation, and the multiple missions of the community college add to the disarray. The community colleges are, at the same time, the place where an increasing number of students complete their pre-baccalaureate general education program. Although the community colleges play a crucial role in higher education, there is sometimes little dialogue or a lot of disagreement between these two critical systems. Indeed, as Harold Hodgkinson points out, "the only people who see these institutions (nursery schools through postgraduate institutions) as a system are the students—because some of them see it all" (1985, p. 1). More educational planning needs to build around the recognition that the students in today's elementary schools are the college students of the future and that these students will often take courses in both a community college and a four-year institution.

Changing Nature of Students. The issue of curricular reform—difficult enough in an educational system that is so diverse, segmented, and decentralized—is made even more complex because our schools are experiencing unprecedented demographic change. White males are already a minority in the nation's schools. By the 1990s, 75 percent of those entering the work force will be women and minorities.

Offering a narrowly prescriptive curriculum does not appear feasible or even well advised. And although it *is* important to provide a coherent curriculum to our students, the demographics of the modern college make this difficult since the educational community is increasingly diverse, nonresidential, and part time. Currently, 40 percent of our students are over twenty-five years old, and only 60 percent attend college full time. Only about one-third of high school graduates go directly to a four-year institution when they graduate. Many students are working adults with family obligations. Women account for well over 50 percent of the twelve million members of the undergraduate student population, and the student body is increasingly diverse, racially and ethnically. More than half the students in our institutions of higher learning are in community colleges. We have seen the future, as Lincoln Steffens said, and the student body is increasingly adult, part time, commuter, pluralistic, and female.

Restoring the Educational Community in a Complex World

The national debate about education is inspiring broad discussion about educational excellence, what it means, and what it requires. As a policy issue, it is being widely discussed in political arenas throughout the nation, and the topic has also captured the public interest. A new spirit of innovation is evident in many quarters. Many states have responded with more financial resources for education, which have often been coupled with increased demands for educational accountability. In general, the most promising responses recognize that effective educational reform is a complicated, multifaceted, long-term business involving rekindling of the spirit as well as refilling the coffers of the educational enterprise.

The learning community reform effort is distinctive in its focus on *structural* barriers to educational excellence, pointing to the structural characteristics of many colleges and universities as major impediments to effective teaching and learning. Large, impersonal, bureaucratic, and fragmented, the American college is often an educational community only in theory. A variety of factors make the notion of meaningful educational community—the root of the word "college"—elusive in many of our institutions. The vision of the collegiate learning community refers to an idealized version of the campus of the past, where students and faculty shared a close and sustained fellowship, where day-to-day contacts reinforced previous classroom learning, where the curriculum was organized around common purposes, and the small scale of the institution promoted active learning, discussion, and individuality. Such a vision remains nostalgic at best, except in small colleges such as Reed, Bard, and St. John's.

Many institutions today have little in common with the campus of the past. With huge enrollments, diverse students and faculty, competing missions, an increasing number of part-time faculty and students, and enormous specialization and fragmentation in the curriculum, many institutions are not experienced by students or faculty as an educational community at all. In many places, the institution can no longer even begin to assume responsibility for creating community.

As the number of full-time and residential students declines, community-creating activities such as late-night dorm sessions, hours spent lingering in a favorite coffee shop, or study break arguments in a library lounge also decline. For many students, the time and spaces for trying out new ideas in the company of peers no longer exists. The college experience is sandwiched between work and family, and the set of classes taken during any given term constitutes the only sustained contact students have with their colleges. *In this environment, the curriculum must now assume responsibilities for building community formerly assumed by the college as a whole.*

Learning communities are a structural response to this fragmentation. They try to establish conditions that promote coherence, community, and a sense of common purpose in an institutional environment otherwise characterized by social and intellectual atomism and fragmentation. In the midst of the pessimism of the national reports, anxiety about "new" students, and the reality of managing large entrenched bureaucracies, reform can seem like an overwhelming task. Learning communities are attractive because they address, in a myriad of ways, issues of curricular coherence, civic leadership, student retention, active learning, educational reform, and faculty development. They are attractive because they chip away at many of these problems all at once without requiring a massive infusion of new money or large-scale institutional reorganization.

Early Roots of Learning Communities: Meiklejohn's Experimental College

Some will surely say that learning communities are not, in fact, a new idea at all—that they are an old idea experiencing a long overdue re-emergence. Others will point to honors colleges and similar enterprises and say that many learning communities already exist. Both claims are true. Learning communities *do* represent an approach well grounded in earlier educational traditions, and they are, indeed, found in some contemporary educational environments. Learning communities are validated by recent pedagogical theory and research on collaborative and cooperative learning, writing, and critical thinking across the curriculum, and feminist theory. The learning community movement is also related to discussions about reforming undergraduate education in general, and general education and the freshman year, specifically. But to go back to the beginning, the structural and pedagogical roots of contemporary learning communities can be traced to the work of Alexander Meiklejohn and John Dewey in the 1920s and the early debates about general and liberal education.

The distinguished philosopher and educational theorist Alexander Meiklejohn wrote in the 1920s with great concern about the increasing specialization and fragmentation in America's colleges and universities. Reading his words in 1989, we are struck by his eloquence and the continuing relevance of his insights. Like many theorists of the time, Meiklejohn was particularly concerned about the relationship between the educational system and democracy. Education is, he argued, a means to prepare students to live as responsible citizens in the contemporary world. He saw college as an important arena for learning and practicing citizenship skills; he regarded the general education curriculum as critical to this task.

Meiklejohn is considered a father to the learning community movement because of his insights about the need to reorganize the structure of the curriculum. His view of the ideal college curriculum was instituted as the Experimental College at the University of Wisconsin in 1927. The first learning community was an integrated, full-time, two-year, lower-division program focusing on democracy in fifth-century Athens and nineteenth- and twentieth-century America. Each civilization was studied holistically through a discussion-centered pedagogy involving the "great books."

The Experimental College curriculum also required students to develop a personal point of view, to connect the ideas in the classroom with the "real world." This proved to be especially effective and was accomplished through a research project:

> It consisted of a paper that students had to produce over the summer between the two years of study. Called the "regional study," it was to be each student's analysis of his hometown or area, based on Lynd's recently published study, *Middletown*. . . . Students' eyes were opened as they looked at their own society with tools they acquired in college, something that traditional education had never asked them to do [Smith and Jones, 1984].

Meiklejohn's curriculum rejected the then prevalent elective system that allowed students great freedom in determining what to study. This system reflected, he thought, "a lack of vision on the part of the faculty" and an abandonment of their responsibility (Miller, 1988, p. 44). He wrote the following:

> Far deeper than any questions of curriculum or teaching method is the problem of restoring the courage of Americans for facing the essential issues of life. How can it be brought about that the teachers in our colleges see themselves, not only as the servants of scholarship, but also, in a far deeper sense, as the creators of the national intelligence? If they lose courage in that endeavor, in whom may we expect to find it? [Meiklejohn, 1932].

Although the program Meiklejohn instituted was based on the great books, he was not a traditionalist in his educational rationale. He was future directed and chose the great books primarily because of their enduring value. This future-oriented point of view was new to educational thinking at the time, as was the notion of a lower-division educational program, which had the creation of an academic community as one of its primary goals. Meiklejohn believed that the unity of his curriculum was achieved from this continuity of context *rather* than through unity of content (Miller, 1988, p. 44).

Meiklejohn is remembered for two distinct though related traditions: (1) his great-books emphasis on the classics, which underpinned the creation of St. John's College and other "great books" schools and (2) his insights about the fundamental importance of structure, curricular coherence, and community. This latter thread, which resulted in the integrated program at the University of Wisconsin, has been recently described in Powell's *The Alexander Meiklejohn Experimental College* (1981).

Tussman's Berkeley Experiment

More than thirty years later, a University of California successor to the Meiklejohn Experimental College emerged. Joseph Tussman, a professor at the University of California at Berkeley and a former student of Alexander Meiklejohn, created a new program and later described it in *Experiment at Berkeley* (1969). Like its predecessor at the University of Wisconsin (1927–1932), the Berkeley learning community effort was short lived (1965–1969), but it too established a model for other educational reform efforts.

Tussman contended that the most significant conflicts in our universities are not necessarily the most obvious ones. Most important, he thought, was the internal tension that resulted from being both universities and colleges at the same time. Tussman wrote eloquently about these two sides of the modern American university:

> The university is the academic community organized for the pursuit of knowledge. It is arrayed under the familiar departmental banners and moves against the unknown on all fronts. Its victories have transformed

the world. The university is a collection of highly trained specialists who work with skill, persistence, and devotion . . . but it pays the price of its success. The price is specialization, and it supports two unsympathetic jibes: the individual specialized scholar may find that, as with Oedipus, the pursuit of knowledge leads to impairment of vision; and, the community of scholars, speaking its special tongues, has suffered the fate of Babel.

The men who are the university are also, however, the men who are the college. But the liberal arts college is a different enterprise. It does not assault or extend the frontiers of knowledge. It has a different mission. It cultivates human understanding. The mind of the person . . . is its central concern. . . . The university (strives) for multiplicity and knowledge; the college for unity and understanding. The college is everywhere in retreat, fighting a dispirited rear guard action against the triumphant university. The upper division dominated by departmental cognitive interests, has become, in spirit, a preparatory run at the graduate school, increasingly professional. Only the lower division remains outside the departmental fold—invaded, neglected, exploited, misused. It is there that the college must make its stand [1969, pp. xiii–xiv].

Tussman believed that a new way of thinking about the students' lower-division general education experience was required to resolve this dualism. Drawing upon Meiklejohn, his solution was to abolish courses as the basic curricular planning units and to see the lower-division curriculum as a "program" rather than a collection of courses. His trenchant analysis of the negative impact of the course remains compelling and central to learning community rationale:

The course forces teaching into small, relatively self-contained units. Horizontally, courses are generally unrelated and competitive . . . no teacher is in a position to be responsible for . . . the student's total educational situation. The student presents himself to the teacher in fragments, and not even the advising system can put him together again. . . . Horizontal competitiveness and fragmentation of student attention are limiting conditions of which every sensitive teacher is bitterly aware. But there is nothing he can do about it. He can develop a coherent course, but a collection of coherent courses may be simply an incoherent collection. For the student, to pursue one thread is to drop another. He seldom experiences the delight of sustained conversations. He lives the life of a distracted intellectual juggler [1969, pp. 6–7].

Structuring the curriculum around programs proved to be, as Tussman predicted, revolutionary in its impact. The programs *required* the re-creation of community among faculty, since programs, unlike courses, could not be usefully taught by a single teacher or from the perspective of a single discipline. These programs asked faculty teams to examine the content and purpose of each offering. They also liberated the planning process, and led to new ways of thinking about how teachers would interact with one another and with their students.

In content, the program at Berkeley was similar to Meiklejohn's, but as Tussman put it, "we were captivated, not enslaved" by the Meiklejohn emphasis. What Tussman did stress was the importance of an emergent, creative process of constructing the curriculum, an insight that flies in the face of many contemporary approaches to educational reform. He said,

> A dominating idea must come first. Without it nothing happens. This has some implications for first-program curricular planning and educational reform. It means, I think, that we should expect nothing, or very little, from academic committees, commissions, or task forces, in the way of real innovation or reform. They are, at best, midwives; they may encourage fertility and even help with the delivery, but they neither conceive nor bear. . . . The curriculum must grow out of a simple idea and be developed by a group committed to the idea [1969, pp. 52–53].

Tussman's ideas took deep root in the state of Washington in 1970, where a group of seventeen planning faculty were designing a new, state-supported "alternative college," The Evergreen State College. Tussman's analysis of the dualistic structure of the American university captured the imaginations of Evergreen's founding faculty. Agreeing that discrete courses were a major obstacle to effective undergraduate education, they decided to design much of the new college around year-long learning communities called "coordinated studies" programs that would be team taught and organized around interdisciplinary themes (Jones, 1981). Mervyn Cadwallader (1984), Evergreen's most influential early dean, argued forcefully for a "moral curriculum" grounded in the humanities and the social sciences that would help prepare students to participate actively in a democratic society. During the third year, thinking that year-long integrated programs could only work in certain subject areas and that the college could attract more students, Cadwallader recommended establishing two colleges at Evergreen, one traditionally structured and the other based on coordinated studies programs. Many faculty rejected this idea. Eventually, the whole college was committed to a coordinated studies curriculum that is thriving at Evergreen today. This curriculum approach became a model for dozens of learning community adaptations in the 1970s and 1980s.

Framers of learning communities have drawn important lessons from Meiklejohn and his successors about the need for appropriate curricular structures and a sense of community and shared values. They also have learned about maintaining innovations in hostile or, at best, indifferent institutional environments. Thus far, the modern adaptations of the Meiklejohn-Tussman approach have proven more enduring than Meiklejohn's or Tussman's original efforts, which did not sustain broad institutional or faculty support.

John Dewey's Influence

John Dewey is another father of learning community work. His contributions had less to do with structure and more to do with the teaching and learning process, especially student-centered learning and active learning. Both Dewey and Meiklejohn were passionately concerned about education and democracy, but interestingly enough, in their lifetimes the two were often noted for their differences. Dewey became associated with an emphasis on the individual and Meiklejohn a proponent for community; Dewey was a pragmatist whereas Meiklejohn was a philosophical idealist. Nevertheless, "Meiklejohn and Dewey arrived at the same terminus: the need to provide education for citizenship, a curriculum of political morality, and a call to teachers to be endlessly experimental rather than doctrinaire" (Cadwallader, 1984, p. 286).

Learning communities often align themselves with Dewey's views about the teaching and learning process. Dewey distinguished between traditional and progressive education by saying that traditional education was "formation from without" whereas progressive education was "development from within" (Dewey, 1938, p. 17). A staunch developmentalist, Dewey believed that "development from within" was the central aim of education and that schools must build on the individuality of each student. Although schools were only one of many places where learning takes place, Dewey regarded them as important ones for building the common culture. He found many schools lacking in terms of furthering student development in the sense that he meant it. Seeing education as "formation from without," many traditional teachers viewed the student's mind as a "cistern into which information is conducted" or "a piece of blotting paper that absorbs and retains automatically" (Dewey, 1933, pp. 261–262). Paulo Freire (1970) later called this a "banking" notion of education in which teachers are depositors of knowledge and students are depositories and in which there is little or no attention to individuality or context.

Dewey thought that this notion of learning was educationally ineffective and inaccurate as a description of how human beings learn. He also thought it undermined individuality, presuming a "uniform immobility on the part of the students." Indeed, the traditional classroom often erected silence as one of its prime virtues, thereby increasing the distance between teacher and learner (Dewey, 1938, p. 63). According to Dewey, the progressive school, by contrast, recognizes that learning is an inherently social process. Students are seen coming to any educational setting with diverse aspirations and prior experiences that must be taken into account in structuring the educational environment.

The type of education Dewey promoted required a close relation between students and teachers, and a different authority relationship based upon an attitude of "shared inquiry." Seeing education as shared inquiry redefines the teacher's role. Instead of being primarily a transmitter of knowledge, the teacher is now a partner in a collaborative relationship. Education is seen as a more open-ended inquiry process rather than a teacher-dominated process of "handing down" knowledge as a finished product.

Often called the father of student-centered and active learning, Dewey believed that education needed to be more purposeful and far less accidental in terms of engaging the learner. The key was to

> [c]onsider the power and purposes of those being taught. It is not enough that certain materials or methods have proven effective with other individuals at other times. There must be a reason for thinking that they will function in generating an experience that has educative quality with particular individuals at a particular time [Dewey, 1933, pp. 45-46].

Dewey criticized traditional education for its fragmented, static quality. With traditional education, he said, "the subject matter is learned in isolation; it was put, as it were, in a water-tight compartment. Where is it now? Probably still stored away in the compartment" (1933, p. 48).

Dewey had a special interest in cooperative and collaborative approaches to education. Properly structured, the educational process should teach important lessons about social control and community life. This, too, alters the role of the teacher who is seen now less as an external authority and more as a leader of group activities (Dewey, 1933, p. 59).

John Dewey framed much of the twentieth-century thinking about the teaching and learning process. Recent scholarship in a variety of fields builds on his work, reinforcing and deepening his observations about the social construction of knowledge, the importance of a developmental perspective, and the value of active learning models (see, for example, Kloss, 1987). Although not connected to Meiklejohn's work at their inception, Dewey's deep insights into the learning process provided a powerful link in the development of today's learning communities.

Conclusion

Learning communities bring together two important threads in the philosophy of education. They draw their curricular structure and some pedagogical insights from Meiklejohn-Tussman-Evergreen experiments and a wealth of theory about the nature of the teaching and learning process from John Dewey. By combining these two threads, learning communities provide one of the most economically viable ways of addressing a variety of educational issues in the complex political economy of today's colleges and universities.

Recent work in such diverse areas as the social construction of knowledge, collaborative learning, writing and critical thinking, feminist pedagogy, and cognitive and intellectual development supports and resonates with the learning community effort. They all stand on the common ground of learning *as* development, the value of building connections, and the power of shared inquiry.

The reasons for actually establishing learning communities have sprung from multiple interests and needs on the part of faculty and administrators. In the national report that recommended establishing learning communities in all institutions, the *Involvement in Learning* study group argued that new research is not needed to address the problems facing higher education today. The research already exists. The National Institute Study Group said that "the quality of undergraduate education could be significantly improved if America's colleges and universities would apply existing knowledge about three critical conditions of excellence: (1) student involvement, (2) high expectations, and (3) assessment and feedback" (Study Group on Conditions . . . , 1984, p. 17). What is needed is courage, commitment, and viable models for implementing these key ingredients. Learning communities represent, we believe, a means of doing just that.

References

Association of American Colleges. *Integrity in the Curriculum: A Report to the Academic Community.* Washington, D.C.: Association of American Colleges, 1985.

Astin, A. *Achieving Educational Excellence: A Critical Assessment of Priorities and Practices in Higher Education.* San Francisco: Jossey-Bass, 1985.

Bloom, A. *The Closing of the American Mind.* New York: Simon & Schuster, 1987.

Bowen, H. "The Reform of Undergraduate Education: Estimated Costs." Unpublished paper presented at the Wingspread Conference on "The Improvement of Undergraduate Education," Racine, Wis., Sept.–Oct. 1985.

Bowen, H., and Schuster, J. *American Professors: A National Resource Imperilled.* New York: Oxford University Press, 1986.

Boyer, E. *College: The Undergraduate Experience in America.* New York: Harper & Row, 1987.

Cadwallader, M. "The Uses of Philosophy in an Academic Counterrevolution: Alexander Meiklejohn and John Dewey in the 1980s." *Liberal Education*, 1984, *70*, 275–292.

Dewey, J. *How We Think*. Lexington, Mass.: Heath, 1933.

Dewey, J. *Experience and Education*. New York: Macmillan, 1938.

Freire, P. *Pedagogy of the Oppressed*. New York: Seabury, 1970.

Gertz, C. "The Way We Think Now: Ethnography of Modern Thought." In C. Gertz (ed.), *Local Knowledge: Further Essays in Interpretive Anthropology*. New York: Basic Books, 1983.

Graff, G. "Taking Cover in Coverage." *Profession*, 1986, *86*, 41–45.

Graff, G. "What Should We Be Teaching—When There Is No 'We?' " *Yale Journal of Criticism*, 1987, *1* (1), 189–211.

Hirsch, E. D. *Cultural Literacy: What Every American Needs to Know*. Boston: Houghton Mifflin, 1987.

Hodgkinson, H. *All One System: Demographics of Education—Kindergarten Through Graduate School*. Washington, D.C.: Institute for Educational Leadership, 1985.

Jones, R. *Experiment at Evergreen*. Cambridge, Mass.: Schenkman, 1981.

Kloss, R. "Coaching and Playing Right Field: Trying on Metaphors for Teaching." *College Teaching*, 1987, *35* (4), 134–139.

Meiklejohn, A. *The Experimental College*. New York: Harper & Row, 1932.

Miller, G. *The Meaning of General Education*. New York: Teachers College Press, 1988.

Powell, J. W. *The Alexander Meiklejohn Experimental College*. Washington, D.C.: Seven Locks Press, 1981.

Ravitch, D. *What Our Seventeen-Year-Olds Don't Know*. New York: Harper & Row, 1988.

Seidman, E. *In the Words of the Faculty: Perspectives on Improving Teaching and Educational Quality in Community Colleges*. San Francisco: Jossey-Bass, 1985.

Smith, B. L., and Jones, R. (eds.). *Against the Current: Reform and Experimentation in Higher Education*. Cambridge, Mass.: Schenkman, 1984.

Study Group on the Conditions of Excellence in Higher Education. *Involvement in Learning: Realizing the Potential of Higher Education*. Washington, D.C.: National Institute of Education, 1984.

Sykes, C. *ProfScam: Professors and the Demise of Higher Education*. Washington, D.C.: Regnery Gateway, 1988.

Tussman, J. *Experiment at Berkeley*. London: Oxford University Press, 1969.

In learning communities, students and faculty members
experience courses or disciplines as complementary and
connected. This chapter describes and compares five major
types of learning community curricular models.

Learning Community Models

A learning community is any one of a variety of curricular structures
that link together several existing courses—or actually restructure the
curricular material entirely—so that students have opportunities for
deeper understanding and integration of the material they are learning,
and more interaction with one another and their teachers as fellow participants in the learning enterprise.

Learning Clusters, Triads, Federated Learning Communities, Coordinated Studies, Integrated Studies—learning community names and models vary from one college campus to another. Yet all these efforts represent
attempts to reorganize and redirect students' academic experience for
greater intellectual and social coherence and involvement. As Chapter
One described, much of this emerging learning community work draws
upon Meiklejohn and Tussman's critical insights about how our curricular offerings are structured, and upon their experiments with rearranging
students' curricular time, space, and intellectual tasks.

In learning communities, students and faculty members experience
courses and disciplines not as arbitrary or isolated offerings but rather as
a complementary and connected whole. These interwoven, reinforcing
curricular arrangements make it possible, then, for faculty and students
to work with each other in less distant, routinized ways and to discover a
new kind of enriched intellectual and social ground.

Although there are significant variations in different institutional
settings, there are basically five major types of learning community curricular models. Table 1, at the end of this chapter, summarizes and compares the principal characteristics of each of five models: (1) linked
courses, (2) learning clusters, (3) freshman interest groups, (4) federated
learning communities, and (5) coordinated studies.

Of course, learning community programs and the way they are implemented vary from one institution to another. Nonetheless, the five learn-

ing community models described here represent a range of generic approaches, a learning community typology that curriculum planners can use to explore their own institution-specific possibilities.

Linked Courses

The simplest form of learning community involves pairing two courses and listing them in the class schedule so that a specific cohort of students co-register for them. The two faculty of the linked courses teach individually, but to some degree they coordinate syllabi and/or assignments. Many courses are linked by the way one course logically builds upon another: writing or speech courses that utilize the content of lecture courses, mathematics courses that support science or business offerings, and theoretical and applications courses that support each other in vocational areas.

Interdisciplinary Writing Program, University of Washington. The University of Washington has been a pioneer in linked courses with its nationally recognized Interdisciplinary Writing Program. The program is a large-scale writing-across-the-curriculum effort, and a learning community endeavor as well. Students are invited to take an expository writing course that is linked to any one of twenty-seven general education lecture courses. The writing and lecture courses carry equal credit: five quarter-hours each. In the early years of the program, the lecture courses were in the social sciences (for example, Introduction to Sociology, Introduction to Political Science) and humanities (Introduction to Art). Recently, however, several natural science courses (in biology, oceanography, and geophysics) have become the basis for writing links, as well as more diverse social science and humanities courses (The Arts of China, Renaissance Florence, Sociology of Deviance, and American Foreign Policy).

In identifying lecture courses to link with writing courses, the Interdisciplinary Writing Program directors find that it takes a lecture class of 200 or more students to yield 20 students interested in a linked writing course. Each year, well over 1000 students take these linked lecture and writing courses, which satisfy either the English composition or "W" (Writing Intensive) course requirements.

Instructors of linked courses work together to generate ideas for writing work based on questions that arise in the lecture course. The two faculty might meet prior to or during the quarter, or the writing instructor might sit in on parts of the lecture course. The writing course specifically develops thinking and writing skills in the disciplinary context, whether it be art history, sociology, or biology. Usually the students in the smaller writing class make up only a small portion of the students in the larger linked lecture course, but they become a small community with a sense of identity and a shared, rigorous academic enterprise.

Combined Courses at Shoreline Community College. Shoreline Community College in Seattle, Washington, has created a similar linked course effort that pairs English composition courses with courses in natural science, social science, and the vocations. In this model, however, the two instructors combine their classes by meeting with their forty students in a daily two-hour block.

Learning Clusters

An expanded form of the linked course model is the learning cluster. Clusters create a broader learning community by linking three or four courses in a given quarter, semester, or year. Again, the courses are scheduled and listed so that a group of students becomes a cohort in the whole cluster. Faculty teach the clustered courses as discrete courses, but for students, the clustered courses are a substantial portion of their course load, or their entire load. At the institutions that offer learning clusters, there are varying degrees to which faculty integrate related material in their clustered courses.

Honors Clusters, Western Michigan University. Western Michigan University has chosen to develop the lower-division portion of its Honors College Program around sets of three clustered courses. For each of their first two years, honors students choose a thematic learning cluster. The clusters consist of two courses limited to twenty-five honors students and one larger lecture course open to a variety of students. The strategy is to build a sense of community among honors students but not to segregate them, thus meeting the familiar criticism that honors classes remove the brightest students from regular classes. Each semester, there are at least four clusters, involving faculty from about a dozen departments around the university. Some examples include

- *Human Nature:* Introduction to Biomedical Sciences, Thought and Writing, and General Psychology
- *Thought and Politics:* Thought and Writing, Principles of Sociology, and Introduction to Political Science
- *Information Processing:* Informational Writing, Finite Mathematics with Applications, and Principles of Sociology.

At first, the Lee Honors College staff chose the cluster themes and courses, obtained agreement from the appropriate faculty, and worked out the scheduling, although departments were also invited to suggest clusters of their own. More recently, faculty members and curriculum committees within departments are beginning to initiate clusters. The Lee Honors College encourages but does not require that the courses be integrated with one another, so the degree of integration varies from one common field trip to semester-long projects based on skills and material from all three courses. Before the academic year begins, the Honors College holds a planning retreat for cluster faculty. Every two or three weeks during the semester, the dean or associate dean of the Lee Honors College convenes these faculty members at lunch to discuss the progress of their courses, to explore ways to further connect courses, and to develop strategies to enrich the integrating experiences.

Learning Clusters at LaGuardia Community College. This commuter school in New York City has pioneered another kind of learning cluster. All day students in the liberal arts Associate of Arts degree program are required to take English Composition in an eleven-credit cluster (see Figure 1) that includes Freshman Composition (English 101), Writing the Research Paper, and course work in social science and/or humanities.

The clusters have thematic emphases appropriate to the character of LaGuardia, a community college with a large cooperative education program and a multicultural student body, largely first-generation Americans. The social science cluster is generally built around the theme of work, and the humanities cluster explores the theme of freedom. There is also an elective business cluster that offers students three required courses for the business program: English Composition, Introduction to Economics, and Introduction to Business. The class scheduling offers the

Figure 1. LaGuardia Community College's Learning Cluster

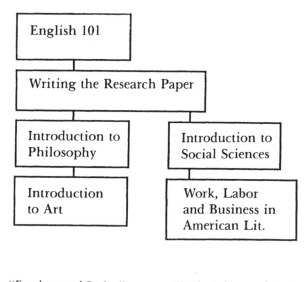

"Freedom and Seeing"   "Work, Labor and Business
                             in American Life"

clustered classes back to back, so commuter students can make the most efficient use of their time on campus (see Figure 2).

At LaGuardia, the cluster size is limited to twenty-six students who travel as a group to all the courses in the cluster. Seven liberal arts learning clusters are offered each year to about 190 students. Because these clusters are required for day students in the AA degree program, they always fill to capacity. The elective business cluster also fills easily because it combines required courses and because eligible students are identified and contacted in a timely fashion with promotional materials.

Faculty at LaGuardia are committed to collaborative planning of the cluster offerings to ensure that students build connections between their courses. The cluster faculty team meets throughout the quarter to discuss how the learning cluster is proceeding.

Babson College Cluster. Babson College, a four-year college of management education with a strong liberal arts component, has developed a similar cluster that links together one required freshman introductory management course, one liberal arts course, and one communications course (either speech or composition). This effort developed out of interests in building closer ties for students and faculty between the liberal arts and the business offerings of the college. The faculty at Babson College use the diagram shown in Figure 3 to illustrate the interrelations in their learning cluster. Although each course meets separately to focus

**Figure 2. Typical Weekly Schedule for Learning Cluster
Courses at LaGuardia Community College**
Work, Labor, and Business in American Society

MONDAY	TUESDAY	WEDNESDAY	THURSDAY	FRIDAY
10:40-11:50 Research Paper	9:20-11:50 Work, Labor and Business in American Literature	10:40-11:50 Research Paper	10:40-11:50 Work, Labor and Business in American Literature	
12:00-1:10 Composition		12:00-1:10 Composition	12:00-1:10 Composition	
1:20-2:30 Intro. to Social Science		1:20-2:30 Intro. to Social Science	1:20-2:30 Intro. to Social Science	

Figure 3. How Babson College's Cluster Courses Share Work in Common

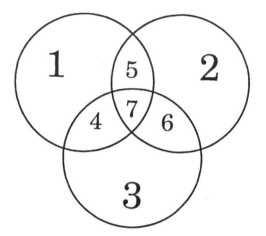

on the subject matter and methods unique to that discipline (Areas 1, 2, and 3), there may be shared meeting times or assignments common to two courses (Areas 4, 5, and 6), or all three courses (Area 7).

Twenty students enroll as a group for each cluster at Babson. Examples include the following:

- *Law in Nature, Society, and Language:* General Management, Introduction to Philosophy, and Speech
- *The Modern European Experience:* Western Civilization, Modern Literature, and Composition
- *The American Myth of Success:* General Management, Composition, and Film.

Cluster faculty agree on common themes, issues, problems, or historical periods to study in the cluster. Some texts are used in all of the courses and there are several common speaking or writing assignments. In a faculty seminar held before the beginning of the cluster, participating faculty discuss which texts to assign and plan both the individual syllabi for their courses and a common syllabus for the learning cluster. In some cases, they prepare to teach a substantial body of new material. Each cluster also features an ongoing faculty teaching seminar in which the faculty discuss both pedagogy and subject matter.

Freshman Interest Groups

The Freshman Interest Group (FIG) model, which also links three courses together, is particularly appropriate to large college or university settings. This model links courses around pre-major topics and has a peer advising component. Each FIG cohort registers for all three courses and travels as a subset of about twenty-five students to larger classes.

The Freshman Interest Group approach is simple and low cost. Most important, this nearly invisible learning community model gives freshmen an immediate support system for their first experience in a large college setting.

University of Oregon. The Freshman Interest Group model originated at the University of Oregon, where the Academic Advising Office conceived the program as a vehicle for advising and for building social and academic community among first-semester freshmen. The office chooses coherent sets of three courses that are typically taken by freshmen and are attractive as foundation courses for a major. Generally, one is a writing or communications course with a lower enrollment level. During the summer, all incoming freshmen receive an invitation to join one of seventeen to twenty "FIGs," which are built around such themes as

- *Pre-Law:* American Government, Introduction to Philosophy: Ethics, and Fundamentals of Public Speaking (see Figure 4)
- *Journalism-Communication:* Comparative Literature, Technology and Society, and Fundamentals of Speech Communication
- *Art and Architecture:* Survey of the Visual Arts, Landscape, Environment and Culture, and English Composition
- *Pre-Health Sciences:* Biology lecture and lab, Psychology, and English Composition.

Most faculty who teach in these linked classes are not expected to coordinate their syllabi or do any co-planning during the semester. Some faculty may attend an inaugural gathering of the Freshman Interest Group and simply introduce themselves and their courses.

The learning community connection for each FIG is provided by a peer adviser. This older student organizes the first meeting of the FIG during New Student Orientation Week and then convenes the group weekly during the semester to explore issues and resources related to student life on campus, form study groups, or just spend some informal time together. The peer adviser receives some upper-division credit in leadership for leading his or her FIG.

University of Washington. The University of Washington has adopted a parallel Freshman Interest Group model and runs about twenty FIGs each year over multiple quarters. The office of the Dean of Under-

Figure 4. University of Oregon's Freshman Interest Group Model

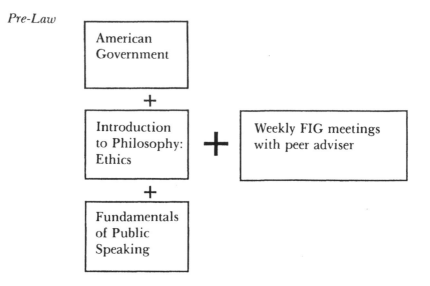

Pre-Law

graduate Studies coordinates the program, with close ties to the General Advising Office, the Office of Minority Affairs, and the Student Athlete Services Program. The FIG coordinator is a half-time teaching assistant who promotes and recruits for the FIG and coordinates the peer adviser program.

Peer advisers are upper-division students, each of whom is usually majoring in the focus of the designated Freshman Interest Group. They receive two credits in general studies (similar to internship credit) for their FIG leadership work. The peer advisers are brought together for an extended orientation and training session before the start of the year. They each meet with their FIG weekly and also meet weekly as a group with the FIG coordinator.

Federated Learning Communities

More complex and academically ambitious, the Federated Learning Community (FLC) model is also appropriate to larger institutions. Although this model builds coherence and community for students, it also provides considerable faculty development. Invented by Evergreen provost Patrick Hill when he was a philosophy professor at the State University of New York (SUNY) at Stony Brook, the FLC model has been transported to several other institutions. It represents an attempt to overcome (for students and faculty alike) the isolation and anonymity of a large research university. Like the Freshman Interest Group model, the FLC "federates" diverse courses around an overarching theme, and invites up to forty students to co-register and travel as a small group within those larger courses.

Examples of Federated Learning Communities are

- *World Hunger:* The Ecology of Feast and Famine, The Economics of Development, and The History of Latin America
- *Issues in Management and Business:* Topics in Management, American Federalism and Intergovernmental Relations, and Ethics in Management
- *Social and Ethical Issues in the Life Sciences:* for upper-division students majoring in biology or psychology and planning careers in the medical and helping professions: General Genetics, The Healer and the Witch in History, and Philosophy and Medicine (see Figure 5).

In addition to the three courses, students also enroll in a three-credit program seminar, a discussion section related to all three courses and led by a Master Learner. A key individual in the FLC model, the Master Learner is a faculty member from a discipline other than those of the federated courses. He or she is expected to become a learner with the students and to fulfill all the academic responsibilities of a student in each course. To do this, Master Learners are relieved of all normal teaching duties Although the Master Learner also convenes the program seminar, she or he, like students, is a co-learner and newcomer to the three disciplines. But the Master Learner's age and training puts him or her in a unique position to assist students in discovering and exploring the integrative and opposing threads and points of view of the three courses.

**Figure 5. SUNY at Stony Brook's Federated
Learning Community Model**

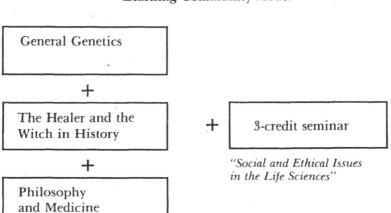

Faculty members who have been Master Learners consistently report how demanding and illuminating it is not only to be a learner in an undergraduate setting again and to reframe their own work in the context of different disciplines but also to engage in a completely new set of relationships with students.

In this learning community model, the faculty-development benefits are immeasurable for both Master Learners and faculty members of the federated courses. As with the Freshman Interest Group model, faculty in the federated courses are not asked to rework their syllabi or coordinate their offerings. However, they do have the benefit of the Master Learner, a mature learner in their midst, who may give them valuable insights from program seminars on how their course material is being understood, interpreted, and applied.

There is, admittedly, a considerable cost in freeing a faculty member for a term or year to become a Master Learner. Several institutions have developed lower-cost adaptations of the FLC model. The Honors Learning Community in the General Honors Program at the University of Maryland has as its Master Learner an outstanding senior high school teacher on a full-time sabbatical fellowship for a year from the Montgomery County, Md., schools. This unique partnership has reaped extensive development benefits for both school and university faculty.

Several schools offer programs in which there are three federated courses and a weekly seminar convened by one of the three federated faculty members. The Stockton State College model, called Federated General Studies courses, links courses in natural science, social science, and the humanities, and does not use a Master Learner. A greater portion of the weekly schedule is devoted to seminar time *within* the federated classes, and the seminar is led by at least two of the three federated faculty. Unlike the Stony Brook program seminar, which draws only on the material in the federated courses, Stockton's seminar is built around additional readings related to the federated course themes.

Coordinated Studies

Of all the learning community models, coordinated studies is the most direct descendent of the Meiklejohn-Tussman experiments. It calls for the most radical restructuring of typical course offerings. Here, members of the learning community—both faculty and students—are engaged full time in interdisciplinary, active learning around themes. Faculty members generally teach *only* in one coordinated study program, and students register for only one coordinated studies program as their entire course load for one or more quarters.

Coordinated studies programs are team-taught by three to five faculty members and involve sixteen credits per quarter. The faculty-student ratio is one to twenty, so that typically a program with three faculty members enrolls about sixty students. The Evergreen State College curriculum is largely built around this model. Many community colleges in Washington state have also adopted this model, offering sixteen-credit coordinated studies programs both in their college-transfer and vocational curricula. Some schools, most notably Seattle Central Community College and Tacoma Community College, are also experimenting with ten- to twelve-credit coordinated studies offerings specifically targeted at part-time adult students.

Coordinated studies programs are diverse in their emphasis and in their modes of delivery. Although students register for coordinated studies programs as a quarter- or semester-long package, credit is generally awarded in terms of discrete, component courses or as lower- or upper-division credit in the component disciplines of the program.

Some coordinated studies programs are highly sequenced and content- and skills-specific. For example, Evergreen's *Matter and Motion* is a year-long program in college calculus, chemistry, physics, and computer applications. Other programs, such as the examples that follow, explore a broader range of disciplines and are more thematic in nature.

- *Science Shakes the Foundations: Dickens, Darwin, Marx, and You:* Students receive disciplinary credit in English composition, physical anthropology, the history of science, and economics.
- *Gods, Heroes, and Humans: Sources of Our Western Traditions:* Credit is awarded in English composition, history, literature, and psychology.
- *Quests:* Credit is awarded in anthropology and developmental writing and reading.
- *Reflections of Nature:* Students receive credit in the visual arts, physics, biology, literature, and computer science.

The full-time nature of coordinated studies breaks open the traditional class schedule with diverse possibilities for scheduling longer blocks of time for extended learning experiences (see Figures 6 and 7).

This opportunity to restructure the schedule, coupled with team teaching by faculty, makes possible a powerful climate for active and interactive learning. Typical coordinated studies programs involve a mix of plenary sessions (lectures, films, or presentations) and small-group work (workshops, seminars, and lab sessions).

"Book seminars," which were central both to the Meiklejohn and Tussman experiments, are the hallmark of most coordinated studies programs. Seminars are extended group discussions of a primary text or article, usually held twice a week. Each faculty member convenes his or her seminar group of about twenty or twenty-five students and acts as a facilitator, encouraging students to develop skills in taking charge of

Figure 6. Typical Weekly Schedule for the Coordinated Study Program "Science Shakes the Foundations"

MONDAY	TUESDAY	WEDNESDAY	THURSDAY	FRIDAY
Prep Day	Lecture 9-11	Seminar 9-11	Lecture 9-11	Seminar 9-11
	Writing Workshops 12-2	Faculty Seminar 12-2	Group Workshops 12-2	Faculty Office Hours 12-2

Figure 7. Weekly Schedule for the Coordinated Studies Program "Data to Information"

MONDAY	TUESDAY	WEDNESDAY	THURSDAY	FRIDAY
8-10 Seminar	9:30 -11 Program Lecture	8-10 Seminar	9-11 Program Lecture	Prep Day
10-12 Math Lecture		10-12 Math Lecture		
	12:30-2:30 Pascal Lecture		12:30-3:30 Pascal Lab	
	2:30-5:30 Digital Logic Lab			

seminar time to dissect the text. Book seminars frequently become the social and intellectual nucleus of coordinated studies as students build an enlarging web of connections among texts, lectures, and the seminars. In addition, most faculty teams set aside time for their own weekly faculty seminar, in which they explore the program texts and questions. Faculty indicate that the faculty seminar discussions are a major highlight of the program. These seminars give them an opportunity for in-depth, challenging intellectual interchange with their colleagues, especially colleagues in different disciplines—an activity lacking in the fragmented, discipline-centered world of academia.

The coordinated studies model offers a highly integrative and intense intellectual experience for students and faculty. The coordinated studies model engages a faculty team in designing and teaching a significant and unified body of material over an extended period of time. Although this structure brings with it a good measure of ambiguity and uncertainty, it is also open to extraordinary possibility and creativity.

Coordinated studies exist within larger, traditional institutional settings, such as the University of North Dakota, and at about fifteen community colleges, many of them in Washington state. Generally, the actual program offerings, as well as the faculty teams, change every quarter or semester. But these shifting offerings are housed and promoted under a learning community umbrella such as "Integrative Studies" or "The Coordinated Studies Program." Starting a coordinated studies program may represent a major commitment by an institution to a new level of cross-disciplinary dialogue.

Learning Communities Within Institutions

With the exception of The Evergreen State College, where the curriculum is built largely around the coordinated studies model, learning communities generally live within a college's regular course offerings. Each of the five major types of learning community programs has been tailored to a particular institution's situation and resources. The precision of these local adaptations has been crucial to the success and sustainability of these programs, but the beauty of these models is that they *are* versatile and dynamic. Indeed, at several institutions, the learning community work was initiated as one model but evolved over time into another. Eastern Washington University launched a Freshman Interest Group model, but interested faculty are now moving the model toward a learning cluster approach with limited class sizes and greater curricular integration. Lesley College's Adult Degree Option Program adopted many features of the Federated Learning Community model, and today that program, as well as several others on the campus, uses the "Integrative Seminar" as a central feature of its curriculum.

By design, learning communities stretch students and shake them out of too-comfortable assumptions about course work or patterns of "doing school." The same can be said for teachers and institutions as well: implementing learning community efforts cannot help but stretch pedagogical and curricular assumptions.

As with any educational innovation, building and sustaining learning communities requires leadership, energy, patience, a willingness to experiment, and perhaps most significantly, a commitment to collaborate across traditional organizational and disciplinary boundaries.

Table 1. Learning Community Models

	Linked Courses	Clusters
Definition	Cohort of students enrolls in two courses, frequently a skills course and a content course.	Cohort of students enrolls in two, three, or four discrete courses linked by common themes, historical periods, issues, problems.
Size of institution	All sizes.	All sizes.
Basic unit of instruction	Two classes usually carrying equal numbers of credits during a given quarter or semester. Students receive separate credit for each of the linked classes. Faculty teaching loads vary: combined, team-taught classes with large enrollments usually make up two courses of the faculty member's teaching load.	Two to four discrete classes (whose content may be tied together in varying degrees) during a given quarter or semester, for which discrete credit is awarded. Faculty teaching loads generally not altered.
Number of students involved	Varies. In linked writing course programs, about 25 students are the whole population of the writing class, but they may represent only a fraction of a larger linked content or lecture class. Larger institutions may offer 40 or more pairs of courses each year.	Varies. Usually 25–30. Institutions may offer one or several different clusters during a given year.

Table 1. *(continued)*

Freshman Interest Groups	Federated Learning Communities	Coordinated Studies
Cohort of freshman students enrolls as a small group in three in-place larger classes and meet weekly with a peer adviser.	Cohort of students and Master Learner enroll in three "federated" in-place courses and participate in a content-synthesizing seminar; faculty of federated courses may offer an additional "core course" designed to enhance program theme.	Multidisciplinary program of study involving cohort of students and team of faculty drawn from different disciplines; taught in intensive block mode to a central theme; teaching is done in a variety of formats (lectures, labs, workshops, and seminars) and all faculty attend all parts of the program.
Appropriate in large institutions.	Appropriate in large institutions.	All sizes.
Three in-place, topically related but autonomous classes during a given quarter or semester, for which discrete credit is awarded. Faculty teaching loads not altered.	Three thematically related but autonomous classes in a given quarter or semester, for which discrete credit is awarded. In addition, credit is awarded for an integrating seminar. Faculty teaching loads (for federated classes) generally not altered; but the Master Learner has no other teaching responsibilities.	The full-time coordinated program is the unit of instruction. Students enroll for entire program and generally cannot break it into subsets. Credit is awarded for equivalent courses, and may or may not be broken out on transcripts. Teaching in the coordinated study generally makes up each faculty member's entire teaching load.
Usually 25–30 students. Typically, institutions run upward of 20 Freshman Interest Groups at a time, usually during the fall. As many as 400–500 students are involved.	20–40 students may be enrolled. Usually one FLC is offered per quarter or semester.	The ratio of faculty to students in a given program is generally 1 to 20. A typical coordinated study involves 3 or 4 faculty and 60 to 100 students. Institutions offer one or more different coordinated studies each quarter or semester; some offer one full-time, 15-credit coordinated studies program and several part-time, 10-credit programs each quarter.

Table 1. *(continued)*

	Linked Courses	Clusters
Faculty roles	Variability in the degree to which faculty coordinate their linked courses. In linked writing courses, the faculty member in writing works closely with the lecture course instructor to generate ideas for writing assignments in the writing course and for writing assignments in the lecture course.	Variability in the degree to which faculty coordinate the clustered courses. Some faculty offer common sessions or assignments; some choose to meet in a faculty seminar before the cluster; some meet during the course of the cluster.
Faculty co-planning	Varies.	Varies from some planning to coordinating syllabi to extensive planning for addressing common themes and issues.
Student seminars	Generally none.	Some courses in the cluster may have a seminar component.

Table 1. *(continued)*

Freshman Interest Groups	Federated Learning Communities	Coordinated Studies
Faculty agree to have their course listed as a FIG offering. They may be invited to attend a beginning-of-the-term social gathering to meet the FIG students.	Master Learner takes the federated courses and core course as a student in areas where he or she has no prior expertise and leads a program seminar, where she or he assists students in synthesizing the material of federated courses, in clarifying issues, and in focusing individual student's interests. Master Learner acts as a mediator of student experiences and provides feedback to federated course faculty regarding their teaching effectiveness. Federated course faculty teach their respective courses; at some institutions, they work together to plan and offer a "core course."	Faculty plan and participate in all aspects of the program; although some parts of a program are run for the entire student cohort (such as lecture), others (such as seminars and workshops) are subdivided into small groups. In some programs, there are internal options to choose from, for example, specific skill or content workshops with designated faculty members.
Generally, no planning or coordination is expected of faculty who teach in the FIG courses.	Federated courses will have some relationship to the FLC theme, but the substance of the courses does not change once federated. If there is a core course, faculty do plan and teach it together.	Readings, lectures, seminars, workshops, and other activities are all planned to explore the program theme. Faculty coordinate the building of themes, connections, and questions, and the ways those connections will be developed through the course of the program. A great deal of planning occurs before the program begins.
Informal discussions are held every week for each FIG with a peer adviser; some of these may develop into more academic seminar-like discussions.	Program seminar is offered only to students enrolled in all three federated courses. The seminar contains no new reading material. The content of the three courses is integrated in the program seminar, where Master Learner assists students in discussing connections and questions they develop from the courses. Intensive writing often occurs.	Weekly or twice-weekly small-group discussions involving about 20-25 students and a designated faculty member who remains with that group for at least a quarter or semester. Special preparation for each seminar is assigned: a book or article, some library research and/or a writing assignment.

Table 1. *(continued)*

	Linked Courses	*Clusters*
Faculty seminars	Occur occasionally at the discretion of faculty.	Occur occasionally at the discretion of faculty, but are a required feature of some cluster programs. Faculty meet to discuss both the cluster's subject matter and pedagogy.
Community-building mechanisms	Shared experience of enrollment in two courses and the reinforcement of skills and content between them.	Shared experience of enrollment in three or four courses and the reinforcement of skills and content among them. In addition, some clusters have common readings, meetings, field trips, or social events.

Table 1. *(continued)*

Freshman Interest Groups	Federated Learning Communities	Coordinated Studies
None.	Variable in scope and frequency. At some institutions, faculty of federated courses and Master Learner meet in seminar to explore theme from their respective disciplines and raise connections and questions.	Weekly gathering of the faculty team to explore content and readings related to their program. This is *not* a time for program logistics. Faculty of some coordinated studies programs invite students enrolled in the program to observe the seminar discussion; this is called a "fishbowl seminar."
Orientation event to meet fellow students, faculty, and the peer adviser; shared experience of enrollment in three courses; weekly meetings with FIG and peer adviser to discuss the course work and share discoveries and problems of adapting to a first term in college. FIGs schedule additional social events and outings on their own.	The seminar's interactive process, the core course, the shared experience, and the multiple feedback loops created by a large cohort enrolled in the same courses combine to build a sense of communal inquiry. Master Learner plays significant role as community-builder and mediator between the federated faculty and the students.	Similar shared experience and multiple feedback loops. Seminar groups generally become smaller subgroups within the community of the whole program. Additionally, community might be built socially and spatially, through dedicated program space, potluck dinners, program field trips, and retreats.

Creating and sustaining a learning community calls for cooperation with a wide spectrum of college personnel.

Making Learning Communities Work: Issues of Implementation and Sustainability

> A prospective, anticipatory view of implementation concentrates on designing policies in advance so they are less likely to fail. In our evolutionary (or learning) view of implementation—implementation as mutual adaptation—a little anticipation and a lot of resilience go a long way.
>
> —Pressman and Wildavsky (1984)

Implementing learning communities provides a rich opportunity and a serious challenge. It can open up new dialogue and build new ties among disciplines and departments. It will also challenge a variety of traditional structures, as some models provide a radically different viewpoint about education, innovative ways of organizing administrative support, more flexible curricular arrangements, and a variety of different teaching tasks. In business, "skunkworks" are deliberately set up within an organization to foster change and are carefully protected as valued countercultural enterprises. We think of learning communities as a kind of "skunkworks" for innovation in higher education.

Taking the First Step

Although academic innovations arise in many quarters, who originates a new learning community program can make a difference. If it is the brainchild of faculty members, there is often a sense of camaraderie, ownership, and contagious zeal. Which faculty initiate the program can also make a difference. Some innovators are appreciated and nourished;

New Directions for Teaching and Learning, no. 41, Spring 1990 © Jossey-Bass Inc., Publishers

others may have reputations as troublemakers or faddists. These perceptions may lend a political aura to the learning community initiative.
Often the learning community is sponsored or created by one subgroup
of the campus, such as the humanities division, the women's studies
program, or the honors program. The sense of ownership and identity
that inevitably unfolds can be a two-edged sword, creating an air of
inclusion and community or exclusion and marginality. If the learning
community faculty considers themselves the "in" group on campus or in
possession of the "New Truth" about college teaching, they may find
themselves isolated from the rest of the campus and the curriculum.

Eventually, ownership of the learning community must be widely
shared among faculty and administrators, and the sooner this happens
the better. If administrators perceive the learning community as isolated
from the "real" work of the institution, sustaining the effort may be
difficult. At one institution, the founding faculty noted:

> There were many barriers to establishing the program. It was designed
> by a tiny group of faculty and developed outside the administration.
> The administration was divided about whether they wanted to have the
> program at all. They were generally skeptical of doing anything differ-
> ent. There were problems with rooms and registering a cluster of
> classes. The life of the project just wasn't in their head and they didn't
> understand the value of doing it. They did finally give the go-ahead
> because we'd worked so hard to develop it. But, of course, we had to do
> all the legwork.

At another institution the issue of broadening ownership also
emerged:

> We are always fighting against provincially oriented and tightly orga-
> nized departments. Some faculty sense this is an elitist program that
> involves only the faculty who are involved in interdisciplinary learning.
> The departmental structure wars against us most because tenure and
> promotion are tied up in those departments.

Many of these pitfalls can be avoided if administrators are involved
at the outset. Administrators who initiate learning communities are often
visionary leaders who see the learning community as a solution to a
problem or a series of problems. They may view the learning community
in a larger context and can often frame the project usefully within the
strategic and financial plans of the institution. Generally, administrators
appreciate learning communities because they contribute to faculty reju-
venation, diversity of student opinion, and active faculty dialogue about
curricular reform.

When administrators launch a learning community, they have, at first blush, enormous power at their fingertips. Canny administrators will build interest, support, and ownership across the campus rather than rely too extensively on a few people who they think are academic innovators and flexible, creative instructors. Ironically, they may find it difficult to involve faculty at first. Teachers may resist changing their courses, often expressing a fear of external control, change, and intrusion into their domain. Administrators need to be sensitive to this fragile yet important aspect of faculty autonomy because it may contain the self-identity of many faculty members.

In general, creating a learning community is complicated and fun for both faculty and administrators, and provides an opportunity for efficient, effective curricular innovation. Although the leadership of the learning community effort is crucial in the beginning, so is finding a permanent place in the life of the institution.

An Administrative Home

Eventually the learning community effort will require stable leadership and an administrative home. As one faculty member in an interdisciplinary program at one large university noted,

> Although it is now well established, initially the program was a step-child, living totally outside any academic department. The courses had interdisciplinary prefixes and were rarely discovered by students. We had to market them like crazy just to let students know they existed. The dean feared that if the program wasn't put under a department, it might be lost during a budgetary downturn, so now we live in the English department and the courses carry English prefixes. This is very helpful in finding students. It's a relief to have the repetitive struggle of recruiting students behind us.

If an administrator acts as the coordinator of the project and assumes responsibilities for logistics, the faculty can concentrate on curriculum development, instruction, and evaluation. Faculty are usually grateful for the assistance, but the downside of this largess is that the faculty may never develop the administrative savvy to manage the learning community. Still, an administrative point person who models a collaborative management style, alerts faculty to curricular quagmires, and smoothes administrative/staff networks is an invaluable resource. Obviously the best arrangement is a partnership of administrators and faculty who meet regularly to consider important learning community issues.

Finding a permanent niche can be difficult for a program seemingly at odds with larger institutional values. At a large university, a member of the faculty said,

> The difficulties impeding a program are linked to faculty mission. Most of the problems arising from the anomalous character of Integrated Studies are fairly trivial, but the problem of recruiting faculty is serious and the recruitment of students suffers too from the freshman advisers being so locked into the departmental conception of the curriculum. They think of general education as a poor second to study in the major.

When a good administrative home is found for the learning community, much can be accomplished quickly and happily. Western Michigan University struggled unsuccessfully for nearly ten years to establish learning communities. Later, when clusters were sited in the Honors College and given clear administrative support, they flourished within a single year. Each institution has its own culture in terms of the most generative place to establish and nurture an innovative enterprise.

Choosing an Appropriate Design and Theme

Critical steps in conceptualizing learning communities involve choosing the appropriate model, selecting the constituent courses, and identifying the program theme. Some questions that can affect the choice of the model concern how the learning community will be connected to specific institutional goals. Will the learning community be instituted for faculty development, as a general education reform effort, or as a writing or critical thinking initiative? What distribution requirements could be usefully linked together? What content courses might benefit from closer articulation with skills courses? How well does the general education course work cohere? Could it be better tied to the major? Are there useful cross-divisional connections to be made? Are there some areas with high student attrition that might benefit from a learning community design?

Cost considerations also influence decisions about what model is viable. As one administrator candidly admitted,

> We were looking for a low-cost model. We run Freshman Interest Groups (FIGs) for about $10,000 per year while the other Freshman Seminar program costs $60,000. The seminars are doing well and they complement the Freshmen Interest Groups, but we can accomplish a great deal with very little money by offering Freshmen Interest Groups.

In determining what kinds of courses and themes to use, it is important to examine natural student groupings and existing curricular possi-

bilities. Since students are concerned about satisfying specific requirements, learning communities need to be formed around courses that are
popular and are important elements of the curriculum. Esoteric courses
usually do not work well in a learning community; general education
courses or pre-major courses do. The challenge for faculty is to focus
their idealism on the possible.

One learning community that was proposed in a college of education
did not enroll well because the faculty did not include the courses required for their own education curriculum. Instead, they chose courses
that they *wanted* the students to take to broaden their major. The students
voted with their feet and went off to the required courses!

This same experience has been repeated elsewhere. Freshman Interest
Groups that are directly titled to connect with student majors, such as
pre-law, pre-health, and pre-engineering, successfully attract students,
whereas those with less clear associations often suffer.

The choice of the learning community design and theme needs to be
made in the context of the institution's goals and what is viable at a
particular time and place. At the first learning community at the University of Maryland, faculty and administrators chose the theme "The City."
When this theme was "market tested" among the students, it received a
thumbs-down rating and was never offered. Two very popular themes,
"Human Nature" and "Science, Technology, and Human Values," sur-
vived transplanting from SUNY at Stony Brook to the University of
Maryland and then to Western Michigan University. These themes have
been successfully attracting students from a variety of majors for more
than ten years. "The Televised Mind" program originating at Bellevue
Community College has a similarly successful record of moving from
one campus to several others in Washington State.

Some schools offer learning communities with different content each
quarter, whereas others have more fixed content. Sometimes the themes
are consistent and the component courses fluctuate. Communication
courses, especially in English composition, are almost invariably included
in learning communities. Essential to meeting distribution requirements,
they also promote the learning community goals of developing student
thinking skills, "voice," and perspective. The University of North Dakota's Integrated Studies Program involves new faculty around slightly
different themes each year, whereas Stockton State College's Federated
Learning Community courses involve the same faculty and consistent
themes. Daytona Beach's Quanta Program is a one-year-long coordinated
studies program whose theme and course components have been the same
for several years. Seattle Central Community College offers as many as
ten thematic programs each quarter; some in English as a Second Language, Allied Health, and Business are repeated offerings, whereas others
are newly created each quarter. Recognizing the benefits of both variable-

and fixed-content programs, one institution, the University of Hawaii at Hilo, is now considering making both "fixed-content" and "variable-content" learning communities part of its general education curriculum. Western Michigan University, LaGuardia Community College, and The Evergreen State College also offer both fixed- and variable-content offerings.

Choosing Faculty

The importance of finding appropriate faculty to teach in the learning community is discussed in Chapter Six. Having at least one good logistics implementor on the teaching team is very helpful to cut the red tape associated with establishing the program. Most institutions also find that some continuity in team contributes to the success of the learning community effort. In many institutions, one member of a teaching team in a given quarter will carry over to the next team the following quarter. Spokane Falls Community College has developed continuity through a faculty "kibitzer," a part-time observer who sits in on the learning community the quarter before he or she teaches in it. Institutions have discovered many different ways to learn how to do collaborative teaching. In Washington state, interinstitutional faculty exchanges provide one vehicle for learning how. Faculty retreats that bring newcomers and veterans together also facilitate sharing of expertise. In many schools, the number of people interested in teaching in the learning community greatly exceeds the positions available. These schools often develop a planning process that is open and encourages rotation.

In a number of learning communities, part-time as well as full-time faculty are involved. Part-timers, who sometimes feel marginal to the institution, are often excellent teachers who can contribute to and benefit from teaching in learning communities. Linked courses, clusters, and Federated Learning Communities are especially appropriate for part-time faculty involvement because they do not require participation in all the component courses. When part-time teachers are involved, it is important that everyone be treated equitably with regard to adequate planning time, compensation, and clear expectations.

Enrollment Expectations and Faculty Load

Much work, hope, and energy can be quickly dissipated if a learning community does not adequately enroll. How many students are required to enable a cluster or coordinated studies program to run is an important and frequent concern. It is wise for administrators and faculty to establish minimal enrollments ahead of time and a contingency plan if those numbers are not met.

Some administrators will allow a new endeavor to proceed even without the required number of students, but most institutions have rigorous requirements in terms of faculty load; these may even be specified in union contracts. If the learning community does not conform to conventional definitions of faculty load, institutional resistance may arise. Faculty need to work closely with administrators to make their program viable from everyone's point of view.

Certain types of learning communities can tolerate load disparities more easily than others. Federated Learning Communities generally have very large enrollments in their federated classes, with only a small subset of learning community students in the program seminar. The subgroup itself usually has an enrollment expectation that can vary a bit without jeopardizing the FLC. Clusters are also fairly flexible. Coordinated studies are more demanding about enrollment levels because the program constitutes a full-time load for two, three, or four faculty members. The important point here is that creative and clear plans concerning faculty load need to be negotiated as part of the creation of the learning community.

In general, learning communities can and do operate at faculty load levels comparable to traditional classes. They simply reconfigure that load—a crucial point in terms of sustainability. Many team-taught interdisciplinary efforts in the 1960s were not viable in terms of usual definitions of faculty load. For example, a small interdisciplinary four-credit course with twenty students might want to have two teachers, but it would generate only eighty student credit hours for the two faculty. In the long run, most institutions could not sustain team teaching with this level of enrollment. By contrast, an eight-credit linked-course learning community with two faculty would have forty students and generate 320 student credit hours, a much more viable faculty load. Learning communities succeed partly because they can operate at more viable enrollment levels. Curricular reconfiguration is the secret. Typically, each teacher carries twenty to twenty-five students, *and* a larger proportion of the students' credit load is in the learning community. The faculty team's overall student credit-hour production is thus reconfigured, but is not dramatically lower than that of their colleagues in conventional classes.

Recruitment, Marketing, and Registration

Vigorous and continuous recruitment of students is required if learning communities are to succeed. There are a number of ways to make students aware of the learning communities. Many institutions prepare booklets or posters that describe the programs in detail. Articles in the student newspaper, radio announcements, and student testimonials also help. A slogan used at the University of Maryland promoted the "learn and earn" approach and illustrated specifically how the courses could be applied toward general education requirements. Some schools devote a special section in their catalog to the learning community effort. Having faculty visit "feeder" courses to introduce and promote the new programs is also useful.

Educating and involving advisers and registration staff in the process of developing learning communities is critical. The staff should be invited to program meetings and seminars as well as planning meetings to get a feel for the programs. Otherwise, misunderstandings can develop. One institution discovered that students who had enrolled in a learning community were later persuaded by their adviser to drop out because he did not agree with the concept. At another institution, the Advising Office mistakenly assumed that the learning community was only for honors students and turned away other prospects. A survey at twelve colleges in Washington indicated that more than half of the students were advised into learning communities by the advising and registration offices. Some schools have planning retreats that involve faculty, key administrators, and advising and registration staff. This helps avoid miscommunication and broadens ownership in the effort.

In the same way that students must be continually recruited to the learning community, registration arrangements must be carefully watched each term. A memo to a registrar or a phone call to the computer center simply is not enough. To get full administrative support requires political savvy, patience, and tact. As one put it, "There were the usual barriers to starting up the program. Registration problems. It's a technical and complicated chore. Anything that threatens the normal technical patterns requires persistence and very delicate negotiations."

Meetings with the registrar and the people associated with the registration process are essential, not because these people are ill-willed or uncooperative but because learning community registration often requires something *different*. Since enrollment limits are often set by the department and then implemented by the registrar, involving the individual who schedules the classes is also a must. In fact, classes are frequently rescheduled to fit the learning community pattern. Building allies in the critical offices on campus facilitates these kinds of adjustments.

Since students usually register for all of the courses in the learning community or for a block of time designated as a coordinated studies program, arrangements need to be made far in advance so that information appears in the class schedule. Sufficient seats must be reserved for subgroups in large classes involved in Federated Learning Communities or clusters, an enrollment limit must be established, and there must be a computer mechanism to code the learning community and monitor course enrollment. At some institutions, students sign up on a separate registration list that is then loaded into the computer. This may be regressive technologically, but it is a reliable way to ensure appropriate enrollment.

Funding, Space, and Teaching Resources

Securing adequate funding for learning communities can be an issue, because the programs are new and often cross established budgetary unit lines. Having vocal and highly placed administrative support is crucial when boundary crossing is required. Special grants helped establish a number of programs. Learning communities at SUNY at Stony Brook, the University of Maryland, Rollins College, Babson College, and the Washington Center were initially assisted by external grants. Still, many learning communities are initiated with few or no new resources. Eight learning communities were established at Western Michigan University and several at Hiram College without outside funding, and in Washington state more than a dozen institutions initiated learning communities with small seed grants of $3000 or less or entirely without outside resources.

Some learning communities' costs are idiosyncratic to certain models. For example, the Federated Learning Community uses a Master Learner position. Again, ingenuity and creative financing are often the best solutions. As mentioned in Chapter Two, the University of Maryland funded its Master Learner through a partnership with the Montgomery County, Md., public schools that established a fellowship program for a high school teacher on sabbatical leave to become a Master Learner for a year. Since the school system already had the sabbatical program, most of the costs associated with the teacher's salary and benefits were already budgeted. The University paid the difference with replacement funds for a part-time faculty member and also provided free tuition for the public school teacher to attend the federated classes. Filling two positions for the price of one, Rollins College uses its learning community coordinator as the Master Learner. Stony Brook presents yet another alternative: it provided a type of sabbatical release time for its Master Learners. Master Learners have also been exchange faculty and graduate students.

One of the biggest problems learning communities face is finding suitable space, or putting it another way, learning communities often require special arrangements. Coordinated studies programs, often involving 50 to 100 students, require both large and small meeting spaces over extended periods of time. Most learning community programs prefer extended meeting times (often three hours) rather than conventional fifty-minute time blocks for teaching. At many schools this makes them, by definition, inconvenient, and inefficient in terms of scheduling space. Federated Learning Communities and clusters also usually need a seminar room in addition to the regular lecture space. Since many learning communities become close-knit groups and students often study together after class, an ideal space would include a small lounge or coffee area dedicated to the learning community. At Daytona Beach Community College, a small, previously unused space in the library quickly became a well-used Quanta study space.

Some of the funding needs for learning communities are especially important in the first year, to orient staff and faculty to the new programs and to recruit students. Many schools make an investment in holding seminars or retreats to discuss the different models and to gain familiarity with the approach. It is also important to recognize that learning communities are cumulative experiences. Activities that create new and different ways for students and faculty to work together add cohesiveness to the community. A small budget for speakers, xeroxing, out-of-class trips, films, or computer materials is useful. Mundane details such as promotional brochures, room size, a lounge, or a nearby copier may seem more like annoyances than important considerations, but these elements are necessary to the functioning of a full-time, integrated learning community program.

Institutionalizing Learning Communities

We have been making the case that the endurance of the learning community effort depends on the institution's strategic understanding of why learning communities are important. All segments of the institution must understand and articulate clear goals that the learning community strives to accomplish. As they turn to issues of long-term sustainability, schools usually establish a home for the learning community, a fairly consistent set of themes or programs, an active group of faculty, and some acceptable administrative procedures. The secret is to ensure that flexibility and ongoing learning continue once the learning community is established.

Another key to sustaining learning communities is creating predictable channels for planning and oversight. At Bellevue Community College in Washington, an effective administrative arrangement now exists for reviewing proposals and selecting future coordinated studies programs. Faculty also receive training on writing proposals and a handbook with clear criteria to address. In this way, diverse groups of faculty are continually brought into the process, thus keeping boundaries permeable and inviting and ensuring broad ownership of the effort.

Establishing a support system for academic innovation that benefits the diverse elements of the college is also important. It is beneficial for administrators to give clear recognition to the learning community effort and to ensure that limits be clearly understood. The reward may be a simple gesture of interest, or it can be more tangible. Money to attend conferences, a graduate assistant to help with tutoring or grading, workshops to educate others about learning communities, publicity on campus, summer stipends for course restructuring, and even merit increases help convey that the work is valued. When all else fails, lunches, teas, or potluck suppers are guaranteed to nourish the project and its participants.

Part of the process of developing learning communities has to do with providing continuous feedback loops and support within the institution. Offering workshops, conferences, and consultants on active learning strategies, writing across the curriculum, and different models for collaboration can aid the process. Bringing many faculty members together also fosters more dialogue, which benefits both the learning community and the traditional curriculum. These efforts also subtly assist in institutionalizing aspects of collaborative education across the institution.

More formal strategies such as time lines, committees, course booklets, faculty training, and curriculum revision and approval also need to be established to fit the decision-making style at each institution. The Evergreen State College establishes its coordinated studies programs in an all-faculty spring retreat, and these choices appear in a yearly catalog. Other institutions use curriculum committees or special learning community planning committees. Some schools purposely embed the learning community in uniform curricular pathways to give the effort more continuity.

Administrators are wise to connect the learning community effort to other campus concerns such as general education reform or a retention initiative, because learning communities can support rather than interfere with these efforts. They can also be congruent with faculty desires to maintain an active research and publication agenda. The "Teacher as Researcher" concept promoted by Patricia Cross (Cross and Angelo, 1985) is an excellent model for internal assessment of learning communities as well as a vehicle for subsequent faculty publications.

Sometimes, consortial arrangements can initiate and sustain learning communities. For example, at the Washington Center for Undergraduate Education, a consortium of thirty-nine colleges and universities based at The Evergreen State College, the director and associate director act as enablers, holding conferences and workshops and working with faculty teams and administrators as they develop learning communities around the state. The Washington Center also brokers faculty exchanges among member institutions, shares information about learning communities in progress, and generally acts as a conduit for supporting and sharing innovation between diverse institutions.

The learning community program should be treated, as much as possible, like other curricular ventures and go through the appropriate ratification channels. This process builds ownership and understanding.

Learning communities need to become part of the landscape, and they need to be seen as a well-researched model and a positive response to a campus issue. Gathering information about other learning communities and higher education reports can help provide a wider context for understanding the various models and purposes of learning communities. As Chapter One points out, learning communities are an idea that has deep roots in the past. Seeing the connections to other programs and earlier traditions helps present learning communities as a thoughtful response to a variety of campus issues, and helps cement their permanent home in the curriculum.

Considerations for the Long Run

Our discussion of learning community implementation is a statement of process, not a recipe for finality. For any innovation to take hold and flourish, the institutional environment must be well prepared and continually tended. Learning communities require time to be refined. Administrators or faculty members who expect instant results or miraculous renewal set themselves up for disappointment. We have observed that learning community programs take at least three years to mature. Because they challenge arrangements at virtually every level of college life, there is a systemic inertia that permits some adjustment but moves steadily back toward the status quo. Learning communities always seem to push against an institutional glacier that grinds away at innovation, smoothing it out and trying to make it like everything else.

In the ideal world, every learning community would have a Great Mother who protects struggling innovators and is fiercely demanding at the same time—one who could move institutional mountains while being sensitive to the most tentative student. Lacking Great Mothers, institutions make do with generous, energetic faculty, excited students, and adept administrators. Ultimately, learning communities work because people care enough about them to invest time and energy in them over the long haul. They stay with the effort.

Learning communities best endure when they fit with the values of the institutional community. They are sustained when the learning community conversations become embedded in the daily academic, social, and political discourse about learning. At their best, learning communities promote an arena for change within the enduring educational establishment. Learning community efforts typically build connections across campus. They also, like all new endeavors, create opposition. Learning communities that welcome and engage the opposition by sharing, explaining, and asking for criticism provide fertile ground for building dialogue across the institution.

Checklist for Implementing Learning Communities

1. What design will be used? In what curricular areas? What themes, if any, will provide the focus for the learning community?

2. Which faculty members will be involved? How will broad involvement be encouraged? Do those who are involved represent the leadership on campus? Who will coordinate the effort in the short and long term?

3. What are the current initiatives on campus? How might learning communities fit with initiatives already under way, such as general education reform, diversity, writing across the curriculum, critical thinking, or others? Are any of the members of the learning community effort connected with these initiatives? Will the learning community be seen as furthering these initiatives?

4. Who needs to be involved with implementing the learning community? Which administrative and support service people should be brought together to discuss implementing the learning community? How can key administrators support this effort? Where are the obstacles?

5. What resources are available to support the project? What is a reasonable time frame if outside funding is needed?

6. How will the learning community be promoted and marketed? How will the students be recruited? What are the appropriate media to use in recruitment?

7. How will the learning community effort be institutionalized? Who will lead the long-term effort in the faculty and in the administration? How will future programs and teams be selected? How will the learning community be evaluated?

8. What kind of feedback loops can be put in place so that the work is evaluated and improved? What kind of mechanisms are there for disseminating efforts within the institution?

Reference

Cross, K. P., and Angelo, T. A. "Classroom Assessment Techniques." In National Center for Research to Improve Post-Secondary Teaching and Learning, *A Handbook for Faculty*. Ann Arbor: University of Michigan, 1985.

This chapter explores how the structure of learning communities shapes the teaching/learning task and describes what kinds of pedagogical adjustments learning communities ask of students and faculty.

Teaching in Learning Communities

Gathered around a table, alternately talking and paused in thought, three teachers plan their courses for a learning cluster they will teach in the coming year. The cluster, organized around the theme of "Human Rights," will contain three courses: Freshman Composition, Introduction to Social Science, and Introduction to Constitutional Law.

A Cluster Evolving

The law professor wants to begin her course with the Bill of Rights. She characterizes her pedagogy as one in which she rarely makes a declarative statement, depending instead on her students to work through a series of questions she poses that arise through open dialogue.

Given the content of the first two weeks of the law course, the social science teacher, a psychologist by discipline, searches for a beginning topic that will contrast dramatically with the Bill of Rights. He has always wanted to teach Elie Wiesel's *Night* and decides that this is the time to explore the authoritarian personality and conditions of life in the absence of human rights. He is accustomed to lecturing and will set out the material logically and systematically in a series of lectures.

The composition teacher, who depends heavily on collaborative learning strategies for her classroom, suddenly remembers that an old friend, a holocaust survivor, had written about her last days at Theirsenstadt, her arrival at Auschwitz, and her escape from the crematory oven. Connecting with the themes and content emerging through these faculty discussions, the composition teacher decides to invite her friend, a veteran teacher of thirty years, to teach a class and to use the visitor's writing about the holocaust as the assigned text.

Eighteen months later, well after the ten-week cluster has ended, students still stop their former teachers in the hallways and talk about how their afternoon with Eva Glaser, holocaust survivor and teacher, helped them reach a more profound understanding of human rights.

It is virtually impossible to participate in a learning community without being transformed in some way. In the above example, the three instructors begin the learning community experience almost naively, adjusting a reading here and there or creating a joint class assignment. However, with the addition of a special visitor, the theme of human rights moves from an abstract idea to an immediate, powerful, and enduring force, igniting the passions of students and teachers. And yet it was more than the special visitor that made this cluster so memorable. What distinguishes the cluster experience is the overall way the structure and content are reorganized to promote coherence, deeper understanding, and dialogue. From the beginning to the end of the quarter, the cluster worked and reworked the theme of human rights, gradually deepening the students' understanding. Through multiple assignments the students develop their skills, but always within a context that makes the writing important. Before Eva's visit, the students worked in collaborative groups to develop questions to ask her, and after her visit, their writing assignments further probed the lessons.

Although usually characterized by extensive preplanning, effective learning communities also leave room to respond flexibly to the unexpected educational opportunities that arise in the course of the quarter. Learning communities are always more than the sum of their constituent parts. They are memorable partly because they are synergistic, coherent educational experiences. Learning communities often have a dynamic quality that arises naturally as a result of putting several teachers together to build a new curriculum. The dynamism also results from the structure, which produces powerful intellectual synergy as well as unpredicted changes in the teaching and learning process. This chapter explores the implications of learning community structure by examining the ways teachers and students make meaning within the learning community.

Structure and the Making of Meaning

Learning communities are, in a fundamental sense, vehicles for the making of meaning. As we pointed out in Chapter One, Tussman (1969) argued that their impact was revolutionary because revising the structure forces teachers to define what is worth studying, and they depend upon collaboration among faculty from different disciplines. In this sense, learning communities require developing a point of view. The learning community structure is critical to this task of making meaning.

Learning communities facilitate the making of meaning in many different ways—through their pedagogy, through their ways of reconceiving content, and through altered conceptions of student and faculty roles.

The learning community structure redefines the context for learning in significant ways. One way to describe what many learning communities do intellectually is to say that they contextualize the disciplines and push both students and faculty to develop a personal point of view about the material and issues being studied.

Learning communities seek to connect, not erase, disciplinary boundaries and to strengthen, not weaken, the teacher-student bond. Students learn that one needs to write competently about issues in biology, chemistry, or sociology, as well as about personal experiences or literature or history. They learn that mathematics is a system of logic that has connections to philosophy and music. They see the concrete manifestations of literary myths in the artifacts and rituals of ancient civilizations. They see that reading philosophy and psychology helps them understand constitutional law and that issues of human rights are not distant, abstract concerns. Even in the most highly integrated models, the disciplines are maintained, but teachers spend less time convincing students of the relevance of the content because the structure and the theme themselves assert the interrelatedness of courses or disciplines.

All learning community models put learning in a context that is larger, more extended, and more coherent than the typical array of classes. However, each learning community does this in its own way. Faculty choose how to use the structure to make meaning of the material, and there is tremendous variability in terms of how different learning communities use the disciplines. In some, disciplinary lines are fairly distinct; in others, they are intentionally blurred. In planning, faculty teams decide where and how students will draw connections and make meanings and how interdisciplinary or multidisciplinary their program will be.

The learning community models differ in the level of involvement they require of students and faculty and in the opportunities they provide for making connections across disciplines. The models also vary in the ways integration takes place. Sometimes the integration occurs around the theme, and sometimes it is more deeply embedded in the structure, the pedagogy, and the roles of the participants. Two of the five models described in this book, Freshman Interest Groups (FIGs) and Federated Learning Communities (FLCs), were designed to create community within regular courses. The intent was to help students make connections across disciplines and with the university without greatly influencing the pedagogical responses of the faculty. These models localize the integrative responses in the specific roles of the peer adviser and the Master Learner, who facilitate community building and integration among the courses. Many learning communities use integrating seminars as the critical integrative element and a kind of catchment area for encouraging the making of meaning and building of new insights and new learning.

Still, the history of even these lower-involvement models suggests that teaching in a learning community, any learning community, affects both faculty and students. Again and again instructors become intrigued by the little communities flourishing in their classes and, on their own initiative, begin a conversation with their colleagues about content and pedagogy that helps to expand the focus of their classes and connect it to others within the learning community.

Linked courses, clusters, and coordinated studies programs all usually require faculty to develop connected or related syllabi, to coordinate assignments, and to plan complementary activities. But even in these models, faculty involvement varies. Levels of coordination and involvement depend somewhat on whether participation in the learning community is a full-time commitment for students and faculty (as in coordinated studies) or is full time for students but only part time for faculty (as in some clusters). The key point is that the level of involvement, coordination, and integration is largely up to the teaching team.

Regardless of the level of initial involvement, the faculty and students in most learning communities inevitably move toward more collaboration. This is so because the structure is a curricular vehicle for intellectual, social, and political synergy. Learning community constituents examine texts, ideas, experiences, and feelings within a group context, and the public nature of this learning compels connection, reflection, and revision. Students develop a sense of their own authority and responsibility to contribute to their own learning, and teachers discover that they do not need to be the final repository of all knowledge. Learning communities enact the social construction of knowledge as it emerges through dialogue and dialectic.

Planning the Learning Community as a Discovery Process

Teachers come to learning communities with diverse personal and professional agendas and a variety of expectations. The learning community structure offers great opportunities for creativity but also a nest of concerns. Teachers wonder how teaching in a learning community is different from "traditional" teaching. They are concerned about preserving the integrity of their disciplines and worry about the time required to participate in the community.

The experience of beginning a learning community is a little like being given a wad of clay that must be worked with and softened before it is pliable enough to take shape. Initial involvement, as with all new endeavors, may be time consuming, and it is up to the team to think through the program and to decide on the desired level of coordination and integration.

Teachers who have never taught in a learning community frequently conserve time and energy by inviting an experienced colleague to sit with them, share experiences, and facilitate the process before the term begins. Identifying themes and primary texts, teachers experience themselves once again as learners, and the learning embedded in the planning process can be enormously invigorating. Faculty members often find themselves becoming more involved than they had anticipated. Their minds become engaged with the possibilities for connection at all levels, and they find themselves tantalized, exasperated, challenged, and rewarded in new and previously unimagined ways.

As with the planning of most courses, the first-time planning of a learning community is the most demanding. Most teachers who join a learning community are willing and even enthusiastic about teaching in this structure again, partly because time spent on one learning community translates to the next learning community. However, a few become overwhelmed and conclude that the demands outweigh the rewards. Many teachers overplan their first learning community. To a certain extent, overplanning is a natural response to a new circumstance—an attempt to control the new and public teaching environment. Most faculty members are concerned about how they will measure up in front of their colleagues. Although overplanning is understandable, it is not really desirable. It can lead to exhaustion and to becoming too rigidly attached to the "new script." It also deprives students of the rigor and joy of making their own connections with the material. One of the central ideas of a learning community is for the whole community to make meaning together. Elements of spontaneity and flexibility are also important because they keep the educational process carefully attuned to where the students are.

Nothing about the process of creating and teaching a learning community is set in stone, and each new learning community is somewhat different. As curricular constructs, learning communities evolve, ripen, and develop. Teams have very different planning styles. Thus, whereas some teams of teachers meet frequently before or during a term and plan exhaustively, others are content with occasional phone contact or a weekly lunch. What is common among learning community participants is the process of discovery and building the community. Students and faculty will constantly wrestle with the questions of how much time to devote to the community, how much they wish to yield in terms of individual needs and schedules, and how hard they wish to push connections with the academic material and with each other. This is the vital, consistent, and persistent process of joining and building a learning community, and it remains, no matter how many times one has participated in such an experience.

Teaching in the Learning Community

Although concerns about time commitment, disciplinary integrity, and level of involvement are embedded in the fabric of learning communities, most learning communities are still made up of regular college classes. They have many features of traditional classes. Visitors to a learning community might observe students listening to a lecture, engaging in a book seminar and debating the meaning of a text, or participating in a small or large group discussion. Students in a learning community may be going on a field trip, visiting the library, keeping a journal, or writing a research paper. Faculty in a learning community use their favorite teaching approaches. Some faculty teams join together more closely than others, combining or contrasting disciplinary perspectives; others experiment more radically.

Many teachers are attracted to learning communities precisely because they provide a context for experimentation and change and an opportunity to share with colleagues and learn from them. They create an arena for discussing and demonstrating a whole range of teaching practices. Because teams of teachers share the same students and are wrestling with the same problems, rich and creative cross-fertilization occurs.

A well-conceived learning community helps students develop a broad array of skills in writing, speaking, critical thinking, group process, and problem solving. Collaborative learning approaches teach students how to work together. Students learn that the whole is, indeed, more than the sum of its parts, as seminar discussions yield new, unanticipated insights on the reading. Teachers foster their students' self-confidence by providing a space for them to think and speak for themselves. Responding to student praise about how well the books are connected, a coordinated studies teacher hastened to reply: "The insights came out of the discoveries and connections you made. We didn't make those connections. We saw some other connections when we started. We didn't see the kinds of connections that you saw and you developed."

To a faculty member accustomed to bearing the sole burden for the class, the joy of a learning community lies in sharing the responsibility with colleagues and students. The arena for learning has been enlarged, and even those teaching their own material in discrete, unchanged courses find themselves acknowledged as working in a larger context. The goals set for learning communities are complex, but these become achievable goals when tackled in concert by a small teaching team in a tangible classroom context.

Students in the Learning Community

The experience of students who travel together in several courses or within a large block of classroom time, sharing their ideas and insights with others, also has an impact on pedagogy. The instructor becomes one of several sources of knowledge. The information he or she provides is received by a group that talks to each other about this information and works to make meaning. Chapter Five indicates that students who participate in learning communities are not exceptional in their views about education. They are, by and large, typical college students, but when they are put in a learning community, their behavior begins to change. They share drafts of papers and revise more freely. They form study groups and pay close attention to sub-groups in the community. They stay engaged. At Western Michigan University, students refer to the cluster they are taking as "my" cluster, claiming ownership in an immediate, personal way.

A sense of responsible citizenship is often present and purposefully cultivated in learning communities. Students feel a community obligation to complete their assignments, attend class, and share their ideas with one another. Those who do not are seen as marginal members. Group processes can be powerful in a learning community, and group norms for tolerance, inclusion, and support are important factors for success. This quality of responsibility is not something students possess initially. When they join a learning community, most students expect to be led. It may be a rude and uncomfortable shock to learn otherwise.

Faculty roles tend to shift as the students become more involved. Faculty members are often amazed at the vitality that a group of students displays. Simple group-process strategies such as a potluck meal or a walk to a museum have an important impact on group life and help students discover personal connections that support their academic work. As the group develops cohesion, students become more ready to take risks such as speaking up in class, asking questions, disagreeing with a fellow student, or writing a dissenting viewpoint. As students develop ownership of "their" learning community, a sort of civic pride arises and students want to do well. As they increasingly gain their voices, enthusiastic students may encourage faculty to move faster or to emphasize different aspects of the course. Sometimes students bring reluctant faculty members into the same room to encounter each other and to discuss issues of common concern. Many faculty credit their students with helping them break out of their own isolated thinking.

An Evolving Coordinated Studies Program

A philosophy teacher is interested in designing a learning community about the Renaissance. Three other faculty will work with him. One will be an exchange faculty member in visual arts from another college. The other two will be in literature and music. After much discussion, the focus of the program changes considerably to accommodate the diverse interests of the four faculty. The team decides to call the program "The

Power of the Person: Looking at the Renaissance." The program will examine changing views of the individual through a comparison of the Italian Renaissance, the Harlem Renaissance, and the Woodstock Revolution in the 1960s.

In the seventh week of the program, the focus turns toward the 1960s. The faculty note that student energy is down and absenteeism is increasing. As a result, they decide to redesign the final portion of the program to increase direct student involvement and commitment. A half-day brainstorming session is held to give everyone in the program the opportunity to share his or her perceptions of the 1960s. The walls are filled with student ideas, associations, and facts about the 1960s. The ideas are then grouped into large clusters—such as civil rights, war and peace, the culture of the 1960s—around which four student groups are organized. The students are given one week to prepare day-long presentations on their topics. Despite the fact that many of the students have family commitments and work part time, they become captivated by the project and dig deeply into the subject. The students scour the community for speakers and information. They probe their families for information. Finally, after many nights of working late, the presentations begin.

The "culture" group presentation goes first. They begin their presentation with a composite video they made with clips from films and television shows that portray the culture of the 1960s. The focus then shifts as the students portray the culture of the 1960s through live theater set in a coffee house. When the presentations are over, everyone is stunned at the extent of the students' work and the level of sophistication in their presentations. Clearly, changing the format of the program was the right move.

Learning community structures set up avenues for intellectual and pedagogical exploration, public learning, and developing responsibility for the wider community. The attitude of shared inquiry and mutual, responsible community often creates a surge of energy that stimulates both students and faculty. Because the content and the players of each learning community are unique and because the community develops in cumulative and synergistic ways, the experience is invariably a process of discovery for everyone. Whether it is a cluster on human rights or a coordinated studies program on renaissance and the power of the person, learning communities provide a powerful vehicle for learning in the context of a community.

Reference

Tussman, J. *Experiment at Berkeley.* London: Oxford University Press, 1969.

Students respond positively to learning community experiences in multiple ways. This chapter reports on what has been learned about the students who enroll in learning communities and their progress and problems in these programs.

Students in Learning Communities: Engaging with Self, Others, and the College Community

The Federated Learning Community has opened doors to getting to know fellow students in an intimate academic community where we could help each other and lean on each other, and feel a personal education in an otherwise impersonal institution. Learning slowly became increasingly fun. Professors became people, there to help you if you needed them—and they had opinions and ideals [Student at SUNY, Stony Brook, in "Technology, Values, and Society" Federated Learning Community].

The fine network of friends and instructors has helped me "define" myself. I have never questioned so many of my beliefs as I have since day one of QUANTA. You all have made me think and rethink about so many ideas. Thank you for waking me up—I might have slept my whole life [Student at Daytona Beach Community College in the QUANTA Coordinated Studies Program].

These are reflections of students at the end of their first experience in a learning community. The themes of engagement with peers and faculty, with ideas, and with one's own learning emerge repeatedly as students across the country reflect on their learning community experiences.

Who are these students? Do they self-select into these collaborative and interdisciplinary settings and then develop already formed interests and abilities in active and collaborative learning? If not, what is it about the learning community experience that engages them? Is it merely a positive, socially reinforcing experience, or do learning communities contribute to greater achievement and competence for performing in undergraduate settings? This chapter discusses what has been discovered about learning community students and their progress and problems in these programs.

Students Who Enroll in Learning Communities

Some learning community programs are designed for specific student populations—for example, honors students, returning adult women, or developmental students. However, most programs recruit broadly from the incoming freshmen population or even from the entire undergraduate student body. Moreover, faculty teaching in learning communities report that the students in their programs are generally typical of students on the campus, and the data support these perceptions.

In its survey of Freshman Interest Group students, the University of Oregon's Academic Advising Office discovered that the FIG students differed from other freshman only in being a little more anxious about making friends and having slightly more elevated expectations about their academic success at the university. FIG students at Eastern Washington University were distinguished by a slightly lower mean high school grade point average than comparable freshmen, although they finished their fall quarter with a slightly higher grade point average.

During the 1987-1988 academic year, the Washington Center for Undergraduate Education surveyed more than 1000 students enrolled in learning communities and comparable traditional classes at twelve community colleges in Washington. Students in both groups were similar in average age and gender breakdown; all were highly oriented to completing a four-year college degree, although this was slightly more true of students in learning communities. Contrary to the findings at the University of Oregon, students in both the learning community and control groups were about equal in their confidence about making friends. On the Measure of Intellectual Development (described later), learning community students scored very slightly higher than students in control groups—indicating, perhaps, a predisposition toward a more interactive, less highly structured, and more conceptually diverse learning environment.

The Washington Center also administered an attitudinal survey and again found only slight differences between the two groups. Learning community students were remarkably similar to those in the control groups in the following dimensions: self-motivation, self-satisfaction, and attitudes toward competition, collaboration, college, faculty, and financial well-being.

Quantitative Measures of Student Achievement and Development in Learning Communities

Student Retention. Student attrition is one of higher education's most pressing concerns. Out of every hundred students who enroll in college, 41 leave without earning a college degree of any kind (Tinto, 1987). Most of them depart during their first two years of college, and withdrawal is highest during the first term. Whether we calculate the losses in wasted resources, in dashed student aspirations, or in workplace unpreparedness, the costs of dropping out are enormous.

One of the strongest selling points for learning communities is their impressive record in retaining students. At the University of Oregon and Eastern Washington University, Freshman Interest Group students have continued into subsequent terms in college at rates consistently and substantially higher than freshmen in general. Beginning to end-of-semester retention rates for Western Michigan University cluster students have been 100 percent. LaGuardia Community College's Learning Clusters have consistently had beginning to end-of-quarter retention close to 90 percent, significant for an urban community college, and coordinated studies programs in Washington community colleges have retention patterns similar to LaGuardia's. For students in learning communities nationwide, beginning to end-of-quarter retention rates average ten to twenty percentage points higher than typical institutional averages. At SUNY at Stony Brook, Federated Learning Community student persistence into the next year in college has run twenty to forty percentage points higher than average.

We believe that the high retention rate in learning communities is partly a function of being enrolled in a program larger than an individual course. Most learning communities require students to register for a large package of credit. That larger package is bound together with multiple and strong social and intellectual threads. These programs raise the expectations and academic stakes as well as provide strong social reinforcement for students. It is not simple, procedurally or psychologically, to drop such an extensive commitment. Even when students in these programs criticize heavy work loads or other stresses in their lives, they acknowledge that their peers and their absorption with the program content keep them from giving up.

Our experience is corroborated by Tinto's (1987) influential book *Leaving College.* He writes about how critical it is for entering students to make a successful transition into the social and academic communities of college. A key factor in retention is the degree to which individual students complete the transition with a sense of congruence, or *belonging*, to the unique academic and social dimensions of the campus. Tinto observes that "Membership in at least one supportive community, whatever its relationship to the center of campus life, may be sufficient to ensure persistence," (1987, p. 68) and that "Departure arises from individual *isolation*, specifically from the absence of sufficient contact between individuals and other members of the social and academic communities of the college" (1987, p. 64).

Learning communities create a unique environment of social and intellectual belonging that is important at any college; they are particularly valuable in large institutions and commuter campuses, where close personal contacts and community making are problematic at best. Learning communities are congruent with good retention practice. While stressing the centrality of intellectual endeavors, learning communities provide close personal contact and continuous social support—a clear message that college need not be a lonely enterprise.

Student Performance. Faculty in learning communities repeatedly speak of high student achievement. Many faculty members observe that in typical classes they see a broad range of students from very poor to very high achievers. In learning community programs, they observe that the spread is much smaller, with many more students doing above-average work. Many faculty also remark that they demand more in these programs, and get more in terms of student perseverance and quality of performance.

Extended comparative studies of student achievement in learning communities relative to that of other students have not yet been done, but our preliminary data indicate that students are higher grade point achievers in these settings. At Eastern Washington University, Freshman Interest Group cluster students entered with slightly lower high school grade point averages than control groups, but they finished their fall quarter with a higher mean GPA. At the end of their freshman year in college, the learning community students' mean GPA remained higher than that of students in control groups. In the biology portion of the FIG cluster at Eastern Washington, the instructor noted that the students' mean GPA in that class was at least .5 higher than in her typical Introductory Biology courses.

LaGuardia Community College conducted several studies comparing achievement of students in Learning Clusters with that of the general student population. Student pass rates in the composition portion of the learning community were about twelve to fourteen percentage points higher than those of the general population. Over several years, about 60 percent of the cluster students were performing at the A or B level, compared with only about 42 percent of the noncluster students (with similar background and similar entering skills). Data gathered by the Washington Center on several coordinated studies at community colleges in Washington state corroborated these findings.

In her follow-up study of Federated Learning Community alumni at

SUNY at Stony Brook, Landa (1981b) found that students' grades went up during their learning community year and continued to rise thereafter.

This information about student performance in learning communities is suggestive, but the factors associated with student attrition and retention and student achievement are complex and highly interwoven. Not only are students learning and performing in contexts very different from typical classes, faculty are *assessing* students in different contexts. Faculty members know individual students far better than they would typically, and in the more team-taught models, they can discuss—and respond to—these students' work, progress, or problems with fellow faculty members.

Student Intellectual Development. Grade point comparisons provide an indicator of student performance, but they do not do justice to the multidimensional development evident in learning community students. These programs generally offer students a more intellectually complex environment. They expose students to topics from the perspectives of different disciplines, teachers, and peers, and ask them to build larger connections and meanings. Most learning communities demand levels of student participation and responsibility not typically found in general education offerings. It is interesting to see whether these socially reinforcing experiences help students develop intellectually as well.

William Perry's scheme of intellectual development in college helps us understand how students function in academic settings and how learning communities foster intellectual development. In *Forms of Intellectual and Ethical Development in the College Years* (1970), he describes how students move through a series of world views, sometimes pausing, sometimes retreating, and how they come to a more sophisticated "making of meaning" about the academic enterprise and about the world. In Perry's view, most students begin college in the stage of "Dualism," seeing the world in absolute, right/wrong or black/white terms. These dualists expect a great deal of structure in classroom settings and see the teacher (the Authority) as the source of the Truth, or at least, the right answers. Then students move into "Multiplicity," where they begin to see issues from multiple perspectives; they acknowledge that teachers are authorities (with a small "a") who provide *methods* for getting to answers and teach not so much *what* to think as *how* to think. These students generally are comfortable with less structured and more interactive, discussion-centered learning settings. Eventually, students leave "Multiplicity" for "Contextual Relativism," where they come to accept the complexities and ambiguities inherent in all knowing. They begin to see that although there can be many answers for each question, some answers are better than others. At this stage, Perry asserts, the hard work begins for students, as they see the need to make their own decisions and commitments and to affirm their own values in a complex world. Perry characterizes these final stages of student growth as "Commitment Within Relativism."

Several studies use the Perry scheme to examine student intellectual development in learning community programs. One involved extended interviews (similar to the ones Perry used in his original studies of Harvard students) of students enrolled in the SUNY at Stony Brook Federated Learning Community. Two other studies used the Measure of Intellectual Development (MID) instrument, an essay-writing test derived from and scored along Perry's positions of intellectual development. The MID was adapted from Perry's work by Knefelkamp (1974) and Widick (1975). One MID study focused on the Honors (Federated) Learning Community at the University of Maryland, and the other involved coordinated studies at several institutions in the Washington Center consortium.

All three studies indicated that students enter learning communities as late "Dualists," a level typical of college freshmen. During a 1987–1988 study conducted by the Washington Center, entering students scored slightly higher on the MID than other students did—perhaps indicating a predisposition toward a more diverse and complex learning setting. However, students in all three studies generally made a significant and unusual leap in intellectual development during their learning community experience. Learning community groups at the University of Maryland and in the Washington Center study exited as early "Multiplists," significantly more advanced developmentally than their counterparts in control groups. Landa's evaluation (1981b) of students in the year-long Federated Learning Communities at SUNY at Stony Brook also found that many students were well along in this multiplistic stage. This indicates that the meanings these learning community students are making of their academic environment are more typical of college juniors and seniors (Landa, 1981b; Gabelnick, Howarth, and Pearl, 1983; MacGregor, 1987).

As with many new educational ventures, most learning community efforts have not launched large-scale evaluation studies. Measures of student retention, achievement, and intellectual development in these programs are all worth gathering, but much time and many resources are required to collect and analyze data consistently over several years. Framing the learning community evaluation strategy must become a high priority of the learning community planning process.

Gathering Qualitative Data About Learning Communities

While quantitative measures provide a picture of student retention and academic achievement, they do not adequately illuminate what happens to students in learning communities: what students value in these programs, what problems they face, and what difference the programs make. Neither do these data provide the kinds of critical feedback that learning community faculty and administrators need to improve these programs. To understand student responses to their learning community experience and to build in ongoing program evaluation many programs build in ways to gather qualitative information. Some programs ask students to keep journals that reflect both their academic work and their sense of personal progress in the learning community. Other programs keep one large journal in which everyone contributes to create a kind of group memory and running log of the learning community's evolution. Still other programs ask students to talk reflectively about their experience at different points along the way, in informal reflective discussion sessions or more formal feedback-giving processes such as the Small Group Instructional Diagnosis process (Redmond and Clark, 1982). In many programs, students are asked to reflect on their learning community experiences through formal writing, whether in written self-evaluations and program evaluations at the end of the quarter or through an assignment to write an essay on "Learning About Learning." Students and faculty alike report that these reflective exercises deepen their learning community experience and help them see the close connection between social and intellectual development. The student quotations in this chapter have been drawn from these kinds of reflective processes on learning communities around the country.

What Students Value About Learning Communities

When students talk and write about their learning community experiences, they remark on their sense of involvement more than anything else—with their peers, their faculty, with college in general, and with themselves as maturing learners. The following themes emerge as students reflect on their experiences.

Friendships and a Sense of Belonging. Learning community students value knowing other students in classes and realize an immediate sense of belonging. As a University of Oregon student put it, "The Freshman Interest Group helped me meet people in what would have been overpowering classes of 200-plus people. It's neat to walk into a big class and see a big group of people you know!"

For freshmen in large institutions, commuter students in community colleges, and rural students whose homes are far away from a residential campus, an immediate circle of friends is seen as a crucial element of the learning community experience. A student at Spokane Falls Community College in the Coordinated Studies Program observed,

> I always envisioned that college was where I was going to make those "friends for life," supposedly that my parents had done when they had

gone to the big schools. . . . Prior to this quarter I hadn't had that at community college. You meet a couple of people in a class and say good-bye at the end of the quarter. In this program, I've made some friends that I'm sure will be my friends for life.

Learning Collaboratively. "Perhaps the most important thing I am learning about learning was that it is easier, and more logical, not to suffer through it by myself. Asking teachers and other students for their ideas or criticism is so beneficial," wrote a Seattle Central Community College student in the "Looking at the Renaissance" Coordinated Studies Program.

Another community college student 3000 miles away echoed this observation:

> When we began writing on the computer I would sit in my chair. Then I began looking at the screen next to me, checking out what Cathy was writing and discussing it with her. Pretty soon, the whole row was comparing notes, and by the end of the quarter, I would get up and walk around to see what my friends were writing, offer them suggestions and get ideas from them [Student at LaGuardia Community College in "American Social History" Learning Cluster].

More than an opportunity for simply bonding with friends, the collaborative academic work in learning communities entails taking something seriously, together. As Anita Landa (1981a, pp. 3-4) commented in her evaluation of SUNY at Stony Brook's Federated Learning Community program,

> Though developing friendships is certainly a legitimate goal of university education, it doesn't happen to be the typical response by students in Stony Brook's FLCs. The respondents are not isolates who have now been blessed with a few intimates. They are people who have suddenly discovered that intimacy has a function in learning: that discussion in a trusting atmosphere is crucial to intellectual discovery and moral honesty; that recognition that professors have opinions and ideals leads to examining one's own viewpoints.

A Stony Brook FLC student remarked,

> I have come to appreciate the importance of academic discussion with my fellow students. I spend much more time discussing what I learn in school with my friends, instead of just discussing school. This interaction has given me a new perspective on my education. I have also realized how much I miss out on in school by not being involved and

dedicated to my work. I have also been inspired to contemplate more on the work I do. I don't just take the easy way out in an assignment.

Intellectual Energy and Confidence. As a result of their engagement, students experience a surge of self-confidence about themselves as learners. Many remark that they felt astonished, at first, that other students or their teachers would even listen to their tentatively offered ideas. Later, they observe that everyone's contributions and responses are energizing, "a kind of special reward for studying." The continuous feedback embedded in these collaborative enterprises develops over the course of the term into a powerful motivating force. As one SUNY at Stony Brook student in the "Social and Ethical Issues in the Life Sciences" program put it:

> I know I can do it from the amount of work I've turned out during the FLC. I went from taking twelve credits and ending up with almost a 3.0 (average), and now I'm taking nineteen credits and I have a good shot at a 4.0. . . . I know that happened to a lot of people in "Social and Ethical Issues." They just took on incredible amounts of work this semester because they felt they could do it. I guess that's a big part of the confidence thing.

Appreciation of Other Students' Perspectives. The discussion and teamwork in learning communities compels students to discover what their fellow students bring to the material, and how and what they think about it. The work of perspective taking is propelled forward when students begin to discover that each of their fellow students brings a special point of view to the learning process. According to a LaGuardia Community College student in an "American Social History" learning cluster:

> We were seventeen to seventy years old, all different races and religions, and had lived in this country all our lives or for only a few months. We shared what we knew. For example, Bernard, our seventy-year-old, hadn't been around in 1877, but he lived through the Great Depression in the 1930s, and he told us about that. It helped us understand what happened to the Grand Army of Starvation.

Such discoveries often lead to a reexamination of one's assumptions about the learning process and the role of peers and development of new sensitivity. As one student put it,

> Up until this program, I've been used to getting the answers from the teachers and things on the board. You know, take good notes, pay good attention to what's in front of you. And pretty much feel cut off—you know, the other students are just learning, they don't have the answers.

But, in this class I've heard some *brilliant* things from other students. I've come to most of my insights through other people. I've really had to look at the way I've been listening to people, and my prejudices in shutting other people's ideas down, and of thinking that I know where the answers spring from [Student at North Seattle Community College in "Revolution and Reaction" Coordinated Studies Program].

Discovering Texts. In learning communities that make the reading and discussion of primary texts a central feature, students build new assumptions and new habits about the role of texts in their learning. As a University of North Dakota Integrated Studies Program student reflected,

I feel I have improved my reading skills. . . . Before my experiences with Integrated Studies I mainly just read a book for pure enjoyment or just to get the facts for a certain test. I never once gave a thought to what the author was trying to say. I have become more interested in books and want to find my own meanings and understandings. I view literature in a totally different way.

Some students discover the power of texts, their authors, and the relationships between them. A North Seattle Community College student wrote in the "Revolution and Reaction" program:

Now what stands out for me more than what we read was what we missed. It's like, Hey, wait! We didn't read Hume! And we didn't read Diderot, and what about the Enlightenment? What about Voltaire? And—the Founding Fathers! I mean, I have never been so moved as reading the few pages in Hannah Arendt when she talks about our Founding Fathers. My Christmas vacation project—I never thought I'd be saying this—is to start reading about the Founding Fathers and America's Revolution.

The Building of Intellectual Connections. The work of drawing meaning from several courses or applying one course's material to another is new, strange, and daunting at first. Many students report that it takes them several weeks—sometimes a whole term—to build their skills and see the power in this kind of learning. But, the discovery is exciting and empowering:

At first, I thought we were studying English, economics, environmental science, and math in a balanced approach. I have come to realize that we have been using English and math to study the dynamics of economics and ecology. In other words, we have been attempting to use two languages to understand the interaction between a social and a biological science [Student at Seattle Central Community College in "The Global Village" Coordinated Studies Program].

Embracing Complexity. As William Perry points out, once students embrace complexity and begin to build the habits and skills of making meaning within that complexity, there is no turning back (1970, pp. 107–108). An intellectual innocence is left behind, and the world becomes a different place. In learning communities, students get inklings of what this kind of intellectual work demands and what it offers. They observe that they "are beginning to see learning in a new light" (1970, pp. 109–133).

A University of Tennessee student in a Federated Learning Community observed, "I never realized the difference between learning and understanding was so great. Learning by itself is something that cannot be used later; understanding allows one to draw and build upon the knowledge one gains, to use that knowledge. I now strive to understand, not to learn."

Sometimes students come to understand and appreciate the intent of the learning community long after it ends. As one alumnus of The Evergreen State College observed,

The integrated studies model . . . is an extraordinary, powerful, and valuable medium. It was in the context of this model that I began to learn new ways of thinking, rather than simply collecting quanta of information as I had (quite successfully) done at the universities I had previously attended. This is the first place I got any *education* at all: where I had the opportunity to integrate bits and chunks of information I was collecting and to synthesize them into a new understanding of the world I live in, of myself, and of my role as a member of society. It's like the difference between collecting a pile of bricks and building a house.

New Perspectives on Their Own Learning Process. College provides an environment for the discovery and definition of self. The learning community acts to enrich that process by creating a supersaturated environment with fertile interplays between the individual and the community, between the individual and ideas, and between the individual and one's own learning process. And new understandings crystalize. As students reflect on their learning community experiences, they almost always talk about new ways in which they see themselves: "The notebook-journal I kept was like the door frame at home with pencil lines and dates on it. . . . I have grown in some ways, and perhaps regressed in others, but I have been able to see the steps I have made" (Student at the University of Tennessee in a Federated Learning Community).

A big revelation came to me in writing seminar yesterday. We were asked to write a dialogue with our work. In the "conversation" I was having with my work, I discovered that I *hate* to be a beginner. I want to be an expert immediately, or not at all. This was a turning point for me, since I am an easy quitter. I always wondered why I could never finish what I started, and why I couldn't make any of my projects turn out. . . . Last night, I thought of the things I want to be good at and the things I want to study. I looked at myself in the mirror . . . and declared myself a novice. I felt a sense of relief, as if I had been unburdened. [Student at Seattle Central Community College in "Looking at the Renaissance" Coordinated Studies Program].

Student Difficulties in Learning Communities

The vast majority of students respond well to learning communities, but not all find the learning community environment their cup of tea. The most frequent complaint has to do with the work load. Students who drop a learning community program are almost always the ones trying to maintain jobs or a demanding intercollegiate sports schedule in addition to schoolwork. Or they are students who registered thinking it would be a "gut course." Many faculty and campus advisers make special efforts to publicize the nature of the reading and writing work loads so students will enter these programs with clear understanding of their demands. In addition, faculty teams frequently develop a program covenant that sets out the expectations of both faculty and students in the learning community.

As noted earlier, many students arrive at college as "Dualists": they are unaccustomed to exploring divergent or opposing viewpoints. Some find diversity or controversy perplexing or frustrating and choose to retreat or adopt an attitude of resentful tolerance. Other students return to old assumptions. In one coordinated studies program, students listening to a discussion about evolution between faculty members in biology and literature interrupted to ask, "Should we know this for biology or literature?" In their enthusiasm at hurtling down new interdisciplinary tracks, faculty must be vigilant not to leave students behind on the platform.

In learning communities that make extensive use of discussions and seminars, there is often a deeply felt anxiety about public learning and a fear, at first, of being exposed. As one student put it,

The first obstacle I encountered was discussion in a group atmosphere. Every time I even thought about something I was going to say, I felt I was dying of a heart attack or suffocation. I decided either to participate or die, whichever came first. Gradually my shyness subsided, and it seemed like people (even the instructor, no less) were interested in my comments. This further inspired me to succeed and to reconsider my former status of stupidity.

Interactive learning situations, especially book seminars, put students into a public and emotionally charged learning situation. Anonymity is virtually impossible. For the shy or less-than-confident student, learning out loud, "doing it live," develops very slowly.

> I feel the only goal I did not reach is my goal to speak out more. I have never been able to speak in front of a group and I do not think I ever will be able to. I figured that if I was ever going to break myself of this . . . it would be through Integrated Studies. But I have failed there. . . . Even so, I have come to accept this fault of mine [Student at the University of North Dakota Integrated Studies Program].

There is the additional risk of bringing up memories of personal experiences that may be painful, confusing, or upsetting. Teachers in these programs soon learn to be sensitive to the complex and delicate nature of a learning environment that often juxtaposes the academic content with the immediacy of personal experience and values.

Collaborative learning formats may present a foreign or even culturally inappropriate learning environment to students whose previous educational experience consisted of passively deferring to authority figures. English as Second Language faculty frequently speak about how some students believe that learning can occur only if the teacher is lecturing, and about how long it takes to convince these students to develop and articulate their own ideas.

There is no getting around it: learning community dynamics, and group relations in particular, are complex. Each learning community becomes a microculture in itself. In the best ones, students feel themselves drawn into its center and reap the intellectual and social benefits. In others, some remain on the margins. We still have much to learn about nurturing the sense of belonging students can achieve in these collaborative settings.

Life After Learning Communities

What happens to students after their learning community experience, when they shift back to a traditional learning environment with more distant and more compartmentalized learning? It is a return to a relative lack of intimacy and intensity and a diminution of the frequent feedback the community learner has come to take for granted:

> Now I'm involved in a lot of very large classes and lecture halls, science classes mainly with giant multiple-choice tests that are somewhat unfair. I don't think that I don't learn as much, but I'm not credited with learning as much as I was in the Federated Learning Community. In the FLC I could just talk—and I could say what was on my mind and express things that I felt were important, and indeed *were* important, I think, and I was helped along and awarded commensurate grades . . . where in these larger classes it's very difficult. I feel I have a much greater understanding of the subject than I'm credited with. It's a bit difficult to swallow [Student at SUNY at Stony Brook, "Technology Values and Society Program" Federated Learning Community].

Nonetheless, students move onward in positive ways. In spite of the less intimate or socially reinforcing atmosphere of traditional class offerings, learning community students take a communitarian spirit with them, striving to be re-creators of community wherever they go. Some work to continue their academic relationships with peers and faculty: learning community alumni register together for classes. They also seek out their learning community faculty by registering for more advanced classes with them or by stopping by to see them informally. Other students search out smaller, more intimate classes, even in the largest universities, and are very clear that they prefer these kinds of settings. Still others become the organizers of collaborative learning endeavors in regular classes.

At Rollins College, one faculty member notes, "Alumni of the Community of Learners Program seem always to be the students who want to get discussions going or who are organizing study groups. They simply stand out in class." At Babson College, cluster faculty have observed that cluster students go on to become the student leaders on campus. Faculty at several Washington community colleges concur: coordinated studies alumni keep reappearing on campus as the "joiners." They are visible and vocal in subsequent classes, and they become active in student groups as well.

Learning Communities as Immersion Experiences

Student perceptions about their learning community experiences and our data paint a compelling picture of the strong and positive impacts of these programs. Are learning community structures, then, a model for reorganizing entire colleges and universities? Certainly elements of these models can be and are being adapted in diverse academic settings. But we agree with Patrick Hill's assertion (1982, 1985) that acknowledging the power of learning communities does not require restructuring the entire academy. The learning community can also be viewed as a rich laboratory—a yeasty environment—to be experienced at least once and *early* in one's college career. The learning community gives students a challenging and supportive immersion in the social and intellectual life of the academy, as well as developing multiple lenses on all that it offers. And it puts students powerfully in touch with the resources of the college, their peers, and themselves.

References

Gabelnick, F., Howarth, J., and Pearl, N. *Facilitating Intellectual Development in University Honors Students.* College Park: University of Maryland Honors Program, 1983.

Hill, P. J. "Communities of Learners: Curriculum as the Infrastructure of Academic Communities." In James W. Hall and Barbara L. Kevles (eds.), *In Opposition to the Core Curriculum: Alternative Models of Undergraduate Education.* Westport, Conn.: Greenwood Press, 1982.

Hill, P. J. "The Rationale for Learning Communities." Paper presented at the Inaugural Conference of the Washington Center for Improving the Quality of Undergraduate Education, Olympia, Wash., October 22, 1985.

Knefelkamp, L. "Developmental Instruction: Fostering Intellectual and Personal Growth in College Students." Unpublished doctoral dissertation, University of Minnesota, 1974.

Landa, A. *Is There Life After Federated Learning Communities?* Stony Brook State University of New York at Stony Brook, Federated Learning Community Program, 1981a.

Landa, A. *Significant Changes: Analysis and Discussion of Fifty-Seven Responses to the Invitation, "Describe the Most Significant Changes You See in Yourself as a Result of the Federated Learning Communities Experience."* Stony Brook: State University of New York at Stony Brook, Federated Learning Community Program, 1981b.

MacGregor, J. *Intellectual Development of Students in Learning Community Programs 1986-87.* Occasional Paper no. 1. Olympia: Washington Center for Undergraduate Education, 1987.

Perry, W. G., Jr. *Forms of Intellectual and Ethical Development in the College Years.* New York: Holt, Rinehart & Winston, 1970.

Redmond, M. V., and Clark, D. J. "A Student Group Instructional Diagnosis: A Practical Approach to Improving Teaching." *AAHE Bulletin,* 1982, *34* (6), 8-10.

Tinto, V. *Leaving College: Rethinking the Causes and Cures of Student Attrition.* Chicago: University of Chicago Press, 1987.

Widick, C. "An Evaluation of Developmental Instruction in the University Setting." Unpublished doctoral dissertation, University of Minnesota, 1975.

Faculty from many disciplines and different kinds of institutions appreciate the associative qualities of learning communities.

Faculty Responses to Learning Communities

My wife kept saying, "You've got to teach this way again; you're a different person this quarter." Subjective and private though this perception is, can one overestimate its significance for a forty-six-year-old teacher approaching his twentieth year of teaching in the same college at the same level? I am exactly the kind of teacher that college administrators shudder at the thought of getting stuck with for another twenty years. I don't blame them. I shudder at the thought of getting stuck with myself!

We have argued that learning community curricular structures offer a successful low-cost, high-yield approach to educational reform. One of the most attractive benefits learning communities offer is a challenging and stimulating opportunity for faculty to work together. Learning communities of seemingly endless variation are prospering in large and small institutions, public and private, and in two- and four-year colleges, and teachers from a broad array of academic disciplines are involved.

Who Teaches in Learning Communities?

Faculty receptivity toward different learning community models appears to vary somewhat according to size of institution and discipline. Existing research offers some clues as to why specific learning community designs and pedagogy may be especially attractive to faculty in certain fields. Dressel and Marcus (1982) indicate that teachers have relatively well-defined orientations toward their disciplinary content, their students, and the educational outcomes, but that these vary substantially from field to field. Kolb (1981, p. 244) points out that "the scientific professions and basic disciplines are predominantly analytical, seeking to understand wholes by identifying their component parts, whereas the social-humanistic fields tend to be synthetic, believing that the whole can never be explained solely by its component parts."

In light of this fact, it is interesting that faculty in the sciences seem especially attracted to clusters, linked courses, and the Federated Learning Community model. These are also the models that are most attractive to teachers in large institutions. Part of the reason may be that these models are more respectful of the standing course offerings and existing sequencing in the curriculum. At the University of Oregon, Freshmen Interest Groups have strong support among several of the noted scientists, especially the biologists; pre-law, pre-med, and pre-health FIGs targeted at pre-professional students are always popular with both students and faculty. At SUNY at Stony Brook, the University of Maryland, and Western Michigan University the FLC and the clusters models have also attracted faculty in the sciences.

The more integrated coordinated-study learning community model seems to be especially attractive to faculty in the humanities and the social sciences—in general, disciplines already predisposed to a more synthetic perspective. Faculty members in English are especially attracted to learning communities, probably because of their stress on active learning methods, cross-curricular writing and thinking approaches, and thematic curricula. Learning communities also offer opportunities for faculty members in English to teach their disciplines, which are too frequently seen as narrow technical and/or service courses, in creative nontechnical ways.

Several of the community colleges in Seattle are running successful learning community programs in developmental education as well as in a variety of vocational areas, including allied health, business, and electronics. Vocational faculty members find that learning communities provide satisfying opportunities to enlarge the context of their work.

In Washington state, the learning community effort draws heavily upon mid-career faculty members for a number of reasons. By choice or circumstance, many have been at a specific institution for a long time. Institutionally secure and highly skilled, they are at a stage in their careers where they feel ready to take new risks as well as make deeper commitments. "When you reach a certain level of proficiency," one of them said, "you get afraid that you're losing your edge if you don't seek new challenges."

A feeling of becoming marginal also nags at many mid-career teachers. Some comment on the unintended but real "disposability mind-set" they see as scores of new faculty are brought in at salaries much higher than those of faculty who have been teaching for years. Part of this phenomenon is that faculty at many institutions are becoming increasingly segmented. There is little relationship between generations and no formal mechanism to build or reinforce a common culture, bridge the cohorts, or take advantage of the talent and wisdom of veterans. As a result, too many are simply waiting out retirement. Learning communities can provide a much-needed vehicle for bridging the generations of teachers by providing a structure wherein veteran teachers can work with newcomers.

In terms of sustainability, it is important that learning communities be led by respected and well-established members of the faculty. This accords legitimacy and respect to the program and encourages other faculty to join in. Many efforts at educational innovation have faltered because they relied too heavily on people with personal or idiosyncratic agendas or people associated with exclusive faculty cliques. This is a hard lesson that a number of learning community designers have had to face. The level of commitment among established faculty is a good indicator of the health and long-term viability of the learning community effort.

Women faculty are highly visible in the learning community effort on almost every campus. Learning communities have features that feminist literature suggests are important, such as cooperation and shared power, development of a personal connection to the material being studied, and an emphasis on the affective aspects of learning (Schniedewind, 1987). The authors of *Women's Ways of Knowing* suggest that women are particularly attracted to what they call "connected knowing" (Belenky, Clinchy, Goldberger, and Tarule, 1986). Perhaps learning communities are oases of sorts that provide connected learning and teaching and a kind of collegiality and "community" that is especially attractive to women.

What Faculty Value About Learning Communities

Surveys of college teachers nearly always cite higher salaries and smaller classes as the necessary ingredients for maintaining faculty vitality, but the problem is more complex than these straightforward but relatively costly solutions suggest. What is really at issue is the overall shape of the work environment, the inherent meaningfulness and value of the educational enterprise, and the nature of our relationships. The current faculty development literature dramatically underestimates our innate curiosity, our thirst for new intellectual challenges, and our ambivalent desire for change.

A variety of factors conspire to make the academic workplace difficult. Higher education is increasingly centralized and bureaucratized, and the scale and fragmentation of many institutions does little to give people a sense of common purpose and personal empowerment. Changing the shape of the workplace in response to these macroforces is no mean task.

Faculty, like most human beings, are ambivalent about change. The regularity of institutional environments reinforces the normal human tendency to see situations and relationships as appropriate and to view innovation with a certain amount of skepticism (Sloan, 1987; Kanter, 1983; Quinn, 1980; Odiorne, 1981; Rogers, 1983; Lindquist, 1978).

Learning communities provide a relatively safe structure for faculty to reframe the work environment and participate in an effort that is "new." Faculty members have a valuable opportunity to become empowered, shape their work, and become colleagues who interact over meaningful issues in pursuit of the common good. This "common good" recognizes our diversity and our creativity, and it evolves organically rather than being handed down through bureaucratic edict. Learning communities allow teachers to alter the structure of the traditional curriculum and give teachers great autonomy to reorganize their teaching *with* their colleagues. Learning communities provide faculty members with new perspective on their disciplines and a new window on pedagogy through which they can directly observe how other skillful teachers think and act. The modeling, mentoring, and learning inherent in this situation are invaluable in faculty development.

A learning community's extended association circumvents many of the real problems that surround traditional faculty development offerings on campuses, which tend to be superficial, exclusively related to research, or detached from a faculty member's disciplinary setting. Clusters and coordinated studies, however, offer a faculty member the opportunity to work with a team in a laboratory for improving teaching that is tangible, with daily opportunities for reinforcement.

Coherence. Lack of coherence is, we believe, a key and overlooked problem in many colleges and universities. For both students *and* faculty, this issue goes much deeper than debates about strategic planning and the content of the curriculum. It extends to the way we structure our time and our relations with one another.

Teachers and students tell us that learning communities provide many types of coherence. Some of the coherence faculty find in learning communities comes from pursuing a single program of study with students over an extended period of time. As a result of working together full time, learning community teachers learn a great deal more about their students and themselves.

As one Centralia College teacher put it,

> The students really became human and so did the teachers. We got an enlarged sense of what the student world is, what goes on in students' minds and all the pain and personal baggage they bring to the classroom. As we got to know one another well, we developed enormous respect for one another. In retrospect, I think I became more a "person"

and less a "teacher" as I learned to bring more of myself to the classroom; I became a much more effective teacher as a result.

Coherence also results from rethinking the curriculum, and participating in learning communities requires faculty to engage in intellectual coherence making. The faculty team developing a coordinated studies program must ask what is important and how various subjects interrelate as they strive to develop a program with a strong intellectual center. The creative act asks a great deal of faculty, intellectually. As one part-time teacher put it,

> As a part-timer I felt a lot of pressure to cover all of the previous content to show full-time faculty that it measured up. We had a hard time throwing out our preconceived ideas and ways of doing things. Controlling our enthusiasm also became an issue; we nearly killed the students at one point with all our planning and enthusiasm. Eventually it worked because we revised the program until it really "fit together" rather than "measured up" and the whole was certainly more than the sum of the parts.

Learning communities allow faculty to reassemble a world that may have become fragmented. A geologist at North Seattle Community College had been lecturing on how the seige works built by Alexander the Great at Tyre altered the natural processes of longshore transport. He was stunned when a student interrupted his excursion into history and testily challenged what a geologist could know about history! This painful reminder that even students overcompartmentalize the curriculum led this teacher to yearn for " . . . an environment where that kind of question wouldn't even occur to anyone."

The Place of One's Disciplines and Venturing Beyond

Through their participation in learning communities, many faculty members enjoy the opportunity to understand their disciplines in a different way. A historian at North Seattle Community College noted,

> I'm coming to understand the strengths and perspectives that are unique to each field. When I lecture, I'm comfortable presenting sweeping themes, categories, and time lines to explain the flow of history. I realize this is a strength, for I see my colleagues fumble with this approach. On the other hand, in our seminars I am impressed with their use of literary analysis, poetic devices, and other perspectives in literature that pass me by. We are all realizing the strengths we bring to our teaching, but we are also introduced to new ways to deal with the same content.

Team teaching using a theme provides a meeting place for new intellectual dialogue and new levels of self-awareness. One faculty member at Seattle Central Community College rediscovered old truths:

> Meeting other faculty in a context of discussing teaching is exhilarating. I'm more enthused about teaching than I've been in years and it's all about rediscovering myself as a learner. Without knowing it, I'd divorced myself from expanding in my field and in my teaching. All the interesting parts of my life were outside the college. I was putting in time so I could be elsewhere. I've learned again something that I knew long ago as an undergraduate: I enjoy learning for its own sake. It makes you feel good and alive. Working with other faculty has been the key to this awakening.

Learning communities provide an important community *structure* for bringing people together in an environment that is otherwise highly individualistic. In many institutions there is little faculty interaction across departmental boundaries. Reward systems, spatial assignments, curricular patterns, and time schedules combine to make faculty interaction, especially around pedagogical or intellectual ideas, rare. Nevertheless, we have found that learning communities can alter patterns of interaction across the institution. As a community college division chair noted:

> There was initial fear and anxiety about teaching with one another, fear about measuring up in front of their peers. But everyone received accolades from their colleagues, and faculty who hardly knew each other before have developed close bonds, good feelings about teaching, and genuine respect for and interest in each other. More than fifty instructors are now involved with our learning community planning group. This quality of community building has been an unexpected and wonderful surprise.

Still, when faculty describe what they value about learning communities, they mostly tell stories about their students. Learning communities allow teachers to invest deeply in their students in a way that has integrity for them. As one teacher at Bellevue Community College put it,

> One of the most striking characteristics was the way the group formed a close-knit community based on care and concern. Many said this was their first experience of such a community and they relished it. From my own perspective as their teacher, I saw students bloom in the kind of environment in which they could be their best possible selves. Certainly one of the strongest arguments for learning communities is that they correct so much of what's not working in education.

Issues Faculty Encounter Teaching
in Learning Communities

Neither the pedagogical assumptions nor the "public" nature of collaborative teaching suit all faculty members. Clearly, some teachers prefer the autonomy of their individual classrooms. On the other hand, a surprisingly large number discover that they are more satisfied and effective when they work with others. As one LaGuardia Community College teacher put it, "When you get more involved with people, there are always more demands. The level of responsibility escalates dramatically." At one large university, a main source of resistance to joining the Integrative Studies Program is the perception that team teaching eats into scholarly time. One faculty member reports, "Faculty who choose to teach in Integrated Studies tend to be more teaching oriented. Others say flatly they need research time. This rings false with some people, but it's very real with others."

In team teaching especially, personal teaching style, the need for control, confidence as a teacher, and maturity are also important factors:

> You need strong people with a solid self-image. You need teachers who can handle being compared with other teachers, sometimes in front of their faces. You need committed and noncompetitive people because there are demands. You have to be willing to meet and discuss what you're doing, and you have to be willing to modify what you are doing.

Teachers oriented more toward student-centered teaching are initially most comfortable with coordinated studies and clusters, though many teachers learn to enjoy the experience. One LaGuardia teacher admitted,

> As a young teacher I felt I needed to be in complete control. I wouldn't have taught in clusters then. I needed to stand up in front of a class with tight control. As I got more confident, I began to loosen up. That's the way it was with most people as they discover collaborative learning.

Learning communities *can* create a good model for working together, but collaborative teaching is a partnership that, like a good marriage, requires respect, hard work, and negotiating skills. Small details such as punctuality and tactfulness often matter a great deal. It is important that potential colleagues be well apprised of each others' pet peeves and personal styles. In some institutions, written faculty covenants outlining expectations have become a useful vehicle for faculty teams to talk through these issues.

Although teaching in learning communities is a satisfying experience for many teachers, a small number of faculty are disappointed with their experience. Sometimes the chemistry of the team is problematic, and personality and organizational differences get in the way. Faculty members may come with different expectations about coverage and evaluation. A program may be unsuccessful because of unrealistic expectations about the students. A team may cast the learning at a level that is too complex for first-year students and cognitive drowning may result. The student mix may also affect the program in any of a number of different ways. Finally, some teachers are disappointed because they join learning communities in the hope of satisfying personal needs that these programs were never meant to address.

To be successful, learning communities depend heavily upon a degree of "fit" among everyone's expectations about the program. These expectations are often extremely high. Students and faculty traveling together on unfamiliar terrain should begin with clear guideposts. Faculty often find that they need to be very clear about the educational rationale and objectives of the learning community. Detailed syllabi, program covenants, and explicit skill-building work for seminars, peer group writing, and group dynamics all help to make collaborative learning more successful. Many programs find that an end-of-the-day "temperature taking and evaluation" improves subsequent dynamics. Utilizing midquarter formative evaluation techniques such as the Small Group Instructional Diagnosis (SGID) is of great value. End-of-quarter reflective interviews and program evaluations also help students and faculty assess their new experience together.

Reconceiving Our Structures and Our Work

Boundary setting is an endemic problem with faculty in learning communities. To a greater or lesser extent, these designs substantially alter traditional faculty definitions of their work. Definitions embodied in the usual "fifty-minute course," "discipline," and "student adviser role" are rather critical guides we depend upon for structuring our work. This changes most learning community environments. Learning communities encourage faculty to re-shape and re-conceive their work. Some faculty become so involved in the learning community experience that they can incur a kind of burn-out.

Given the high stimulation of the more integrated learning community models, it is not surprising that many faculty and students experience "post–learning community depression" when a program ends. One instructor at Bellevue Community College reported that returning to the traditional classroom "felt like being tossed into an icy lake after crawling out of a warm bed." Many report that the adjustment to the traditional classroom is hard and lonely. "In the end," one reported, "this made many of us even more frustrated knowing that, despite the party line, given our current work load standards, our students in traditional classrooms simply are not getting a good education."

The positive response to "learning community nostalgia," as it is called at one institution, has generally been to find ways of integrating some of the learning community approach into traditional classrooms, to maintain the friendships and intellectual conversations initiated there, and to actively support the learning community effort and its spin-offs in the institution.

Many aspects of learning community theory and practice can be directly transferred to the traditional classroom, and nearly all involved report that they learn new teaching methods and refine old ones, often gaining a new view of themselves. One instructor reported that "teaching in front of other instructors made me look at myself the way the students look at me, and I started to think about defining outcomes more explicitly. I don't think I paid much attention to that before."

Writing about the overall experience at Bellevue Community College, one instructor notes that "probably the single most important thing each of us took back was an almost evangelical commitment to the idea and practice of student-centered learning." Learning communities are often powerful vehicles for the practice of collaborative learning and the promotion of various forms of active learning. For the faculty, their impact on pedagogy is usually critical and long lasting.

Learning Communities and the Academy

In his book *Embracing Contraries: Explorations in Learning and Teaching*, Peter Elbow (1986, p. 264) writes compellingly about the need for the academy to play both the "doubting game" and the "believing game":

> As intellectuals, we have a special role as doubters. A culture needs people who stand back and view critically what the majority assumes, who question society and its values . . . [but] doubt caters too comfortably to our own natural impulse to protect and retain the views we already hold. . . . Doubting is the act of separating or differentiating and thus correlates with individualism. . . . Belief involves merging and participating in a community; indeed a community is created by— and creates—shared beliefs.

In an important sense learning communities are a "public believing game" set in a highly individualized academic culture more accustomed to playing the "doubting game." Our experience with learning communities suggests that they enable faculty to find different ways of thinking about what promotes effective educational reform, excellence in teaching and learning, and collegiality. Clearly, there is a deep hunger among faculty members for more meaningful collegial relationships and more effective "conversational structures" in our institutions.

What faculty value in learning communities is that they tap a reservoir of energy in our institutions that comes from what John Dewey called the "power of human association." A centripetal impulse in a society increasingly beset by the twin forces of bureaucratization and individualism, learning communities are a powerful associative response to many of the educational needs of our times. And, as Patrick Hill (1985) put it,

> on our campuses we need associative educational structures that build significant educational dialogue into the *real* time and *real* space, the regular time of the work day.
>
> You may say, "Doesn't the university or the college have the time and space to learn from each other? Isn't it set up that way?" And my answer is, "No. It is set up to discourage communication across boundaries and to discourage people from having time to talk to each other." Fundamental to all of this work is building—into the ordinary time and space of the people within the institution—the opportunity to work together, to learn from each other, and to release the powers of human association.
>
> If you state it simply, this objective seems obvious and easy to achieve. Because we have been living in a too isolated and atomistic way, you must go about it in a dogged fashion. If you create these opportunities and make them real and reward them, then a tremendous amount of creativity comes forth and people start to learn again and to feel excited about their work.

References

Belenky, M. F., Clinchy, B. M., Goldberger, N. R., and Tarule, J. M. *Women's Ways of Knowing: The Development of Self, Voice, and Mind.* New York: Basic Books, 1986.

Dressel, P. L., and Marcus, D. *On Teaching and Learning in College: Reemphasizing the Roles of Learners and the Disciplines in Liberal Education.* San Francisco: Jossey-Bass, 1982.

Elbow, P. *Embracing Contraries: Explorations in Learning and Teaching.* New York: Oxford University Press, 1986.

Hill, P. "The Rationale for Learning Communities." Keynote address delivered at the Inaugural Conference of the Washington Center for Improving the Quality of Undergraduate Education, The Evergreen State College, Olympia, Wash., Oct. 22, 1985.

Kanter, R. M. *The Changemasters.* New York: Simon & Schuster, 1983.

Kolb, D. "Learning Styles and Disciplinary Differences." In A. W. Chickering and Associates, *The Modern American College: Responding to the New Realities of Diverse Students and a Changing Society.* San Francisco: Jossey-Bass, 1981.

Lindquist, J. *Strategies for Change.* Berkeley: Pacific Soundings Press, 1978.

Odiorne, G. S. *The Change Resisters.* Englewood Cliffs, N.J.: Prentice-Hall, 1981.

Quinn, J. B. *Strategies for Change: Logical Incrementalism.* Homewood, Ill.: Irwin, 1980.

Rogers, E. M. *Diffusion of Innovations.* New York: Free Press, 1983.

Schniedewind, N. "Feminist Values: Guidelines for Teaching Methodology in Women's Studies." In Ira Shor (ed.), *Freire for the Classroom: A Sourcebook for Liberatory Teaching.* Portsmouth, N.H.: Boynton Cook, 1987.

Sloan, T. *Deciding: Self-Deception in Life Choices.* New York: Methuen, 1987.

The growing interest in learning communities resonates with preoccupations in higher education.

Learning Communities, Curricular Reform, and the Future

We began by tracing the foundations of learning communities to the Meiklejohn-Tussman focus on the necessity for coherently structured curriculum and to Dewey's insistence on the importance of the teaching and learning process. More recently, feminist and collaborative learning theories, along with other initiatives, have enriched and extended these earlier ideas. They ask us to acknowledge and hear the existence of multiple voices and to value the experiences of cooperation and coordination. These strands all combine in the learning community movement, a comprehensive response to the plethora of problems in higher education associated with fragmentation and isolation.

At a time when higher education appears to be moving away from a sense of shared purpose and community, learning communities offer a way to maintain the balance between striving for oneself and contributing to the common good. In *Habits of the Heart*, Robert Bellah and his associates explore a similar unhealthy tilt toward individualism in contemporary American society. Reflecting on much earlier observations by Alexis de Toqueville in *Democracy in America*, Bellah points to

> The mores . . . "habits of the heart" . . . [that] . . . helped to form American character. . . . [Toqueville] also warned that some aspects of our character—what he was one of the first to call "individualism"—might eventually isolate Americans one from another and thereby undermine the conditions of freedom. . . . We are concerned that this individualism may have grown cancerous—that it may be destroying those social integuments that Toqueville saw as moderating its more destructive potentialities, that it may be threatening the survival of freedom itself [Bellah and Associates, 1986, p. vii].

Learning communities are one way of redressing this imbalance. By promoting integration and cooperation, they counteract the isolating tendencies of education and the curricular "dis-integration" that results when knowledge is compartmentalized into competing disciplines and isolated courses. For both faculty and students, learning communities help develop the cooperative values and inclusive intellectual habits essential to counterweigh individualism with the communal spirit.

Learning community models also facilitate sharing knowledge and solving problems, thus enriching the presentation of the traditional liberal arts and furthering the goals of general education. Cross-disciplinary learning communities link the liberal arts and humanities with technology and enrich professional studies. Thematic linkages join vocational and preprofessional studies with an appreciation of the historical, cultural, and artistic expressions of related human activities. Anthropology, sociology, and ethics in a learning community help professionals examine pragmatic and moral issues embedded in the technicalities of their practice.

Because traditional courses often fail to communicate the connections between disciplines, learning may seem arbitrary and whimsical to students. Learning communities help students forge the connections in their writing, thinking, and knowing, paralleling initiatives that promote writing and thinking across the curriculum. Basic skills and English as a Second Language students apply newly acquired skills in communities that help them establish relationships and relate concepts from one area to another. Learning communities encourage teachers to experiment with their presentation of content and the ways they and their students make meaning. For all these reasons, learning communities are soundly compatible with contemporary pedagogical reform efforts.

Learning communities are strong vehicles of empowerment, promoting active learning. At the developmental level or as part of an honors program, learning communities can become a delivery system for academic excellence. Students rise to the occasion of learning communities: they perform better, accomplish more, drop out less. By modeling the idea that disciplines need to work together to explore issues thoroughly, the learning community experience helps them develop breadth of vision and mutual respect. Students have the invaluable experience of learning from each other and working as equals in exploring common issues. The data support student evaluations that attest to the social and intellectual empowerment of learning communities, whose lessons reach beyond the classroom.

The National Board for Professional Teaching Standards, formed by the Carnegie Corporation, recently defined teachers as "members of learning communities who can work in collaboration with other teachers in collegial settings to improve schoolwide learning" (Fiske, 1989).

Learning communities support this definition by breaking down the barriers among faculty trained in different disciplines and among faculty at different stages in their careers. They offer an alternative to an educational environment where loyalty to one's discipline separates, excludes, and isolates. Instead, learning communities give teachers a chance to stretch into a multidisciplinary or interdisciplinary approach. As an organizational model that promotes communication and exchange, learning communities emphasize the primacy of teaching in a context of intellectual growth and development. Engaging in common endeavors and seeking to understand issues from broader perspectives revitalizes a faculty.

Learning communities can also serve as revitalizing agents on campuses as a whole, since creating and sustaining a learning community demands that all elements of a college—students, teachers, administrators, and support staff—work together. Communities depend on this diverse group of individuals coming together for the overriding purpose of the college experience: educating the same students together.

Not to be ignored is the economic attractiveness of the learning community effort. Viewed purely from the standpoint of diminished resources for educational revitalization, it has many advantages. It uses people and resources already in place. The start-up costs are low, and, in terms of dollars, the effort is quite efficient.

Since colleges and universities mirror the demographic realities and "habits of the heart" of American society, they share its pressures and problems. The tensions of pluralism that have existed so long outside the academy now exist within it. In "The Recoloring of Campus Life: Student Racism, Academic Pluralism and the End of a Dream," a thoughtful analysis of the roots of the new racism on campus, Shelby Steele (1989, p. 55) concludes:

> Integration has become an abstract term today, having to do with little more than numbers and racial balances, but it once stood for a high and admirable set of values. It made difference second to community, and it asked members of all races to face whatever fears they inspired in each other. I doubt the word will have a new vogue but the values, under whatever name, are worth working for.

Although American society is still dangerously stratified along racial, ethnic, and class lines, social interaction promoted by learning communities provides a context for students from all ethnic groups to learn together. They help students get a sense of themselves among others in an environment of mutual dependency, respect, and cooperation. As Clifford Gertz (1985, p. 16) suggests:

> To see ourselves as others see us can be eye-opening. To see others as sharing a nature with ourselves is the merest decency. But it is from the far more difficult achievement of seeing ourselves amongst others . . . a world among worlds, that the largeness of mind, without which objectivity is self-congratulation and tolerance a sham, comes.

In order to use their learning for the good of humankind, our students must be taught cooperation and sharing. The growing number of homeless people and the growing hole in the ozone layer result from bankrupt policies that sacrifice the common good for individual comfort. Solutions to the problems of our time require multiple points of view, a variety of skills and understandings, an acknowledgment of interdependence, and mutual respect. We must support educational endeavors such as learning communities that give us these skills and values.

Habits of the Heart celebrates the kind of creative discussion between individuals and groups that guarantees the perpetuation of a culture:

> So long as it is vital, the cultural tradition of a people—its symbols, ideals, and ways of feeling—is always an argument about the meaning of the destiny its members share. Cultures are dramatic conversations about things that matter to their participants. . . . American culture remains alive so long as the conversation continues and the argument is intense [Bellah and Associates, 1986, pp. 27-28].

Both our society and our educational communities depend on these conversations. Insofar as they create arenas where faculty and students can contribute to the richness of this dramatic conversation, our colleges encourage and contribute to the continued existence and evolution of American culture. Learning communities provide such an arena and help develop the critical consciousness that enriches the argument.

Cooperation, coordination, and communication—these are the keystones of our culture. As educators, we help shape the behaviors that shape public behavior. Teaching is a political act; regardless of our disciplines, whatever we teach, and whatever our individual political points of view, our overriding obligation is to educate a citizenry.

Because of this, we have a special obligation to seek antidotes to the forces that fragment and isolate us. We need to create programs that bring us together, structurally in some cases, intellectually and emotionally in others. For the common good, education must offer a space for "conversations about things that matter." Learning communities are one way that we may build the commonalities and connections so essential to our education and our society.

References

Bellah, R. N., Madsen, R., Sullivan, W., Swidler, A., and Tipton, S. *Habits of the Heart: Individualism in American Life.* New York: Harper & Row, 1986.

Fiske, E. B. "Lessons." *New York Times,* April 5, 1989, p. B12.

Gertz, C. *Local Knowledge: Further Essays in Interpretive Anthropology.* New York: Basic Books, 1983.

Steele, S. "The Recoloring of Campus Life: Student Racism, Academic Pluralism and the End of a Dream." *Harper's,* February 1989, pp. 47–55.

*People, networks, and literature support institutional efforts
to implement learning communities.*

Resources on Learning Communities

The reader interested in exploring learning communities will find a body
of literature available, but more important, a group of people who are
willing to share their experiences. This chapter begins with a list of the
major learning community programs and contact people. It also includes
three major learning community networks. The final section provides a
brief bibliography.

Learning Community Model Programs and Contact People

Learning communities are now found in many different institutions.
The following list is organized around the different learning community
models, with names of contact people who can provide more detailed
information about their institution's program. We know that our list is
incomplete: there are dozens of programs that we have not mentioned
and indeed, might not even know about. We invite readers to send us
additional information.

Linked Writing Courses

Joan Graham, English
Interdisciplinary Writing
Program, GN-30
University of Washington
Seattle, WA 98195
(206) 543-0758

Marie Rosenwasser
Division Chair, Humanities
Shoreline Community College
16101 Greenwood Avenue North
Seattle, WA 98133
(206) 546-1741

Carole Bulakowski, Director
Learning Assistance Center
College of Lake County
19351 West Washington Street
Grayslake, IL 60030-1198
(312) 223-6601

Learning Clusters

Kelly Lynch
English Department
Babson College
Wellesley, MA 02157
(617) 235-1200

Paul Marshall
Everett Community College
801 Wetmore Avenue
Everett, WA 98201
(206) 259-7151

Jerri Lindblad
Department of English
Frederick Community College
Frederick, MD 21701
(301) 694-5240

Roberta S. Matthews
Associate Dean
for Academic Affairs
LaGuardia Community College
31-10 Thomson Avenue
Long Island City, NY 11101
(718) 482-5674

Faith Gabelnick, Dean
The Carl and Winifred Lee
Honors College
Western Michigan University
Kalamazoo, MI 49008-3899
(616) 387-3230

Jeff Chertok
Sociology Department
Jois Child
Geography and Sociology Departments
Eastern Washington University
Cheney, WA 99004
(509) 359-7929
(509) 359-2433

Freshman Interest Groups

Jack Bennett
Joe Wade
Academic Advising
and Student Services
University of Oregon
Eugene, OR 97403-1217
(503) 686-3211

Fred Campbell, Associate Dean
Ken Tokuno, Director of Special
Undergraduate Programs
Arts & Sciences GN-15
University of Washington
Seattle, WA 98195
(206) 543-5340

Federated Learning Communities

James McKenna, Chair
Federated Learning Communities
State University of New York
Stony Brook, NY 11794
(516) 246-8611

Jack Lane, Professor of History
Communities of Learners Program
Rollins College
Winter Park, FL 32789
(305) 646-2000

University Honors Program
0110 R. Lee Hornbake Library
University of Maryland
College Park, MD 20742
(301) 454-2532

Martha McKenna
Weekend Learning Community
for Adults
Lesley College
29 Everett Street
Cambridge, MA 02138
(800) 999-1959

Jamie Cromartie
Natural Sciences and Mathematics
Stockton State College
Pomona, NJ 08240
(609) 652-4413

Faith Gabelnick, Dean
The Carl and Winifred
Lee Honors College
Western Michigan University
Kalamazoo, MI 49008-3899
(616) 387-3230

Coordinated Studies

Barbara Leigh Smith
Academic Dean
The Evergreen State College
Olympia, WA 98505
(206) 866-6000

Richard Zelley
Cindy Avens
Co-directors
QUANTA Program
Daytona Beach
Community College
P.O. Box 1111
Daytona Beach, FL 32015
(914) 255-8131

Gerald Lawrence
Pat Sanborn
Co-directors
Integrated Studies Program
P.O. Box 8012
University of North Dakota
Grand Forks, ND 58202
(701) 777-3622

Ron Hamberg, Dean
Seattle Central Community
College
1701 Broadway
Seattle, WA 98122
(206) 587-4164
(SCCC has approximately ten
learning communities each quarter in academic transfer, developmental, and vocational areas,
including allied health, ESL, and
business.)

R. Edmund Dolan, Dean
Bellevue Community College
3000 Landerholm Circle S.E.
Bellevue, WA 98007
(206) 641-2041
(Bellevue offers learning communities in its academic transfer curriculum and developmental
education area.)

Ron Johns, Dean of Instruction
Spokane Falls Community
College
W. 3410 Fort George Wright Drive
Spokane, WA 99204
(509) 459-3538
(Spokane Falls offers learning
communities in its academic
transfer and developmental areas.)

Lucy Charnley, Dean
North Seattle Community College
9600 College Way North
Seattle, WA 98103
(206) 527-3722
(North Seattle offers learning communities in its academic, transfer, vocational, and developmental curriculum.)

Richard Guaraski, Director
The Freshman Program
St. Lawrence University
Canton, NY 13617
(315) 379-5909

Coordinated studies programs are also in place at the following community colleges in Washington state: Edmonds, Lower Columbia, Spokane, Skagit Valley, Tacoma, and Yakima Valley. In addition, Fairhaven College at Western Washington University is based upon collaborative learning. The Washington Center for Undergraduate Education (listed below) is a consortium acting as a facilitator and clearinghouse for learning community work in Washington; it may be contacted for information and will match inquiries with appropriate programs.

Networks

Three networks support learning community and other collaborative efforts and work together to share information and resources.

Collaboration in Undergraduate Education (CUE) is the oldest of the networks, formed in 1983 with support from the Fund for the Improvement of Undergraduate Education (FIPSE) and the Association of American Colleges (AAC). In 1985, CUE became one of the "action communities" of the American Association for Higher Education to help organize its annual conference and continues to promote collaborative approaches to teaching and learning through workshops, panel presentations, consulting, and a variety of publication efforts. The mailing list is national and contains approximately 600 names. For information, write:

Collaboration in Undergraduate
Education (CUE)
Bill Whipple
Honors Program
University of Maine
Orono, ME 04469
(207) 581-3263

For mailing list, write:
Karen Romer
Associate Dean of Academic Affairs
Brown University
Providence, RI 02912

The Center for Collaborative Learning was funded by FIPSE in 1987 and is located at Lesley College. The center serves as an informal clearinghouse for information and people associated with collaborative learning and learning communities. It holds periodic conferences on collaborative learning and related issues. It is creating a directory of model programs and a packet introducing approaches to assessment appropriate to collaborative learning contexts. The Center has available an extensive and growing bibliography on collaborative learning and learning communities.

Center for Collaborative Learning
Anita Landa
Lesley College
29 Everett Street
Cambridge, MA 02238
(800) 999-1959

The Washington Center for Improving the Quality of Undergraduate Education is a state-funded consortium of 39 colleges in Washington state. Based at The Evergreen State College, whose curriculum is built around the coordinated studies model, the Center is a faculty and curriculum development network focusing on active and collaborative learning and the development of learning communities. The Center holds conferences, brokers faculty exchanges, provides technical assistance, and manages a seed-grant program. It also publishes a quarterly newsletter and occasional monographs.

Washington Center for Undergraduate Education
Barbara Leigh Smith and Jean MacGregor
The Evergreen State College
Olympia, WA 98505
(206) 866-6000

Resources on Learning Communities

The following represent major works on learning communities:

Gabelnick, F. "Curriculum Design: The Medium in the Message." In P. G. Friedman and R. C. Jenkins-Friedman (eds.), *Fostering Academic Excellence Through Honors Programs.* New Directions for Teaching and Learning, no. 25. San Francisco: Jossey-Bass, 1986.

Gamson, Z. F., and Associates. *Liberating Education.* San Francisco: Jossey-Bass, 1984.

Hill, P. J. "The Incomplete Revolution: A Reassessment of Recent Reforms in Higher Education." *Cross Currents,* 1975, *24,* 424–443.

Hill, P. J. "The Ethics of Helping: A Comparison of the Role of Self-Reliance in International Affairs and Pedagogy." *Metaphilosophy*, 1981, *12* (2), 181-205.

Hill, P. J. "Communities of Learners: Curriculum as the Infrastructure of Academic Communities." In J. W. Hall and B. L. Kevles (eds.), *In Opposition to Core Curriculum: Alternative Models of Undergraduate Education*. Westport, Conn.: Greenwood, 1982.

Hill, P. J. "A Deweyian Perspective on Higher Education." *Liberal Education*, 1984, *70*, 307-313.

Hill, P. J. "Inter-Generational Communities: Partnerships in Discovery." In R. M. Jones and B. L. Smith (eds.), *Against the Current: Reform and Experimentation in Higher Education*. Cambridge, Mass.: Schenkman, 1984.

Jones, R. *Experiment at Evergreen*. Cambridge, Mass.: Schenkman, 1981.

Landa, A. *Is There Life After Federated Learning Communities?* Stony Brook: State University of New York, Federated Learning Community Program, 1981. (Available from The Center for Collaborative Learning, Lesley College.)

Landa, A. *Significant Changes: Analysis and Discussion of Fifty-Seven Responses to the Invitation, "Describe the Most Significant Changes You See in Yourself as a Result of the Federated Learning Communities Experience."* Stony Brook: State University of New York, Federated Learning Community Program, 1981. (Available from The Center for Collaborative Learning, Lesley College.)

MacGregor, J. "Intellectual Development of Students in Learning Community Programs, 1986-87." Unpublished paper, The Washington Center for Undergraduate Education, Olympia, Wash., 1987.

Matthews, R. S. "Learning Communities in the Community College." *Community, Technical, and Junior College Journal*, 1986, *57* (2), 44-47.

Matthews, R. S. "Social History and the Community College Student." *Community Review*, 1988-1989, *9* (1-2), 35-40.

Meiklejohn, A. *The Experimental College*. New York: Harper & Row, 1932.

Miller, M. "On Making Connections." *Liberal Education,* 1982, *69* (2), 101–107.

Smith, B. L. "The Washington Center: A Grass Roots Approach to Faculty Development and Curricular Reform." *To Improve the Academy,* 1988, *7,* 165–177.

Smith, B. L., and Hunter, R. "Learning Communities: A Paradigm for Educational Revitalization." *Community College Review,* 1988, *15* (4), 45–51.

Smith, B. L., and Jones, R. (eds.). *Against the Current: Reform and Experimentation in Higher Education.* Cambridge, Mass.: Schenkman, 1984.

Tussman, J. *Experiment at Berkeley.* London: Oxford University Press, 1969.

Resources on Collaborative Teaching and Learning

There is a large literature on collaborative learning. The following bibliography represents major works:

Bouton, C., and Garth, R. Y. (eds.). *Learning in Groups.* New Directions for Teaching and Learning, no. 14. San Francisco: Jossey-Bass, 1983.

Bruffee, K. A. "Liberal Education and the Social Justification of Belief." *Liberal Education,* 1982, *68,* 95–144.

Bruffee, K. A. "Writing and Reading as Collaborative or Social Acts: The Argument from Kuhn and Vgotsky." In J. N. Hays and others (eds.), *The Writer's Mind: Writing as a Mode of Thinking.* Urbana, Ill.: National Council for Teachers of English, 1983.

Bruffee, K. A. "Collaborative Learning and the Conversation of Mankind." *College English,* 1984, *46,* 635–652.

Bruffee, K. A. "Liberal Education, Scholarly Community and the Authority of Knowledge." In *Interpreting the Humanities.* Princeton, N.Y.: Woodrow Wilson Foundation, 1985. (Reprinted in *Liberal Education,* 1985, *71,* 231–239).

Bruffee, K. A. "Social Construction, Language, and the Authority of Knowledge: A Bibliographical Essay." *College English,* 1986, *48,* 773–790.

Bruffee, K. A. "The Art of Collaborative Learning." *Change,* March/April 1987, pp. 42-47.

Castelucci, M. F., and Miller, P. *Practicing Collaborative Learning.* New York: CUNY College of Staten Island, 1986.

Cohen, E. G. *Designing Groupwork: Strategies for the Heterogeneous Classroom.* New York: Teachers College Press, 1986.

Gere, A. R. *Writing Groups: History, Theory, Implications.* Carbondale: Southern Illinois University Press, 1987.

Johnson, D. W., and Holubec, E. *Circles of Learning: Cooperation in the Classroom.* (2nd ed.) Edina, Minn.: Interaction Book Company, 1986.

Maruyama, G., Johnson, R. T., Nelson, D., and Skon, L. "Effect of Cooperative, Competitive, and Individualistic Goal Structures on Achievement: A Meta-Analysis." *Psychological Bulletin,* 1981, *89,* 47-62.

Palmer, P. *To Know as We Are Known.* New York: Harper & Row, 1983.

Romer, K. T. "Collaboration: New Forms of Learning, New Ways of Thinking." *Forum for Liberal Education,* November/December 1985, *8* (2).

Romer, K. T. *Models of Collaboration in Undergraduate Education.* Providence, R.I.: Brown University, 1985.

Slavin, R., Sharan, S., Kagan, S., Hertz-Lazarowitz, R., Webb, C., and Schmuck, R. *Learning to Cooperate, Cooperating to Learn.* New York: Plenum, 1985.

Treisman, U. "A Study of the Mathematics Performance of Black Students at the University of California, Berkeley." Doctoral dissertation, University of California, Berkeley, 1985.

Whipple, W. "Collaborative Learning: Recognizing It When We See It." *AAHE Bulletin,* 1987, *40* (2), 3-7.

INDEX

ORDERING INFORMATION

NEW DIRECTIONS FOR TEACHING AND LEARNING is a series of paperback books that presents ideas and techniques for improving college teaching, based both on the practical expertise of seasoned instructors and on the latest research findings of educational and psychological researchers. Books in the series are published quarterly, in Fall, Winter, Spring, and Summer, and are available for purchase by subscription as well as by single copy.

SUBSCRIPTIONS for 1990 cost $39.00 for individuals (a savings of 20 percent over single-copy prices) and $52.00 for institutions, agencies, and libraries. Please do not send institutional checks for personal subscriptions. Standing orders are accepted.

SINGLE COPIES cost $12.95 when payment accompanies order. (California, New Jersey, New York, and Washington, D.C., residents please include appropriate sales tax.) Billed orders will be charged postage and handling.

DISCOUNTS FOR QUANTITY ORDERS are available. Please write to the address below for information.

ALL ORDERS must include either the name of an individual or an official purchase order number. Please submit your order as follows:
  Subscriptions: specify series and year subscription is to begin
  Single copies: include individual title code (such as TL1)

MAIL ALL ORDERS TO:
  Jossey-Bass Inc., Publishers
  350 Sansome Street
  San Francisco, California 94104

DATE DUE

MAR 0 3 2012	

LB 2361.5 .L43 1990

Learning communities

Made in the USA
Lexington, KY
23 February 2011